ADULT EDUCATION
AND THE STATE

Adult education has frequently assumed a political role in society and also has itself been regarded as a social movement. This book, however, is the first systematic attempt to analyse if from the perspective of political theory. The book seeks to locate the education of adults within current political theory – something which has become even more relevant since the Conservative government of the UK has adopted an interventionist approach to education.

The book starts from a historical perspective, examining the relationship between adult education and civil society, and explores theories of the state. It discusses the concept of democracy and shows that there are a variety of different forms with which the education of adults might be related. The idea of citizenship is also examined, and it is suggested that the education of adults might be regarded as a citizenship right which is being lost to all citizens as a result of current government policies. Peter Jarvis also looks at the relationship between liberal adult education and a civilised society, suggesting that its provision is one of the symbols that a society is moving on the long journey towards creating a civilised society. The final chapter illustrates the existence of utopian thought in radical adult education.

Peter Jarvis has published widely in the field of the education of adults and is a frequent speaker/lecturer on the subject throughout the world. His book *Adult Learning in the Social Context* was awarded the Cyril O Houle World Award for Adult Education Literature, and he has also been awarded a Japan Society for the Promotion of Science Fellowship to study the education of adults. He is currently Professor of Continuing Education in the Department of Educational Studies at the University of Surrey, and an honorary adjunct professor of adult education at the University of Georgia, USA.

ADULT EDUCATION AND THE STATE

Towards a politics of adult education

Peter Jarvis

London and New York

First published 1993
by Routledge
11 New Fetter Lane, London EC4P 4EE

Simultaneously published in the USA and Canada
by Routledge
29 West 35th Street, New York, NY 1001

© 1993 Peter Jarvis

Typeset in Stempel Garamond by
Michael Mepham, Frome, Somerset
Printed and bound in Great Britain by
Biddles Ltd, Guildford and King's Lynn

British Library Cataloguing in Publication Data
A catalogue record for this book is available
from the British Library.
ISBN 0–415–06532–1

Library of Congress Cataloging-in-Publication Data
Jarvis, Peter, 1937–
Adult education and the state / Peter Jarvis.
p. cm.
Includes bibliographical references and index.
ISBN 0–415–06532–1
1. Adult education and state—Great Britain. I. Title.
LC5256.G7J37 1993
374'.841—dc20   92-37660
                                                CIP

CONTENTS

PREFACE

The history of the education of adults is both complex and paradoxical: liberal adult education began in civil society as a religious concern which grew into a social movement but, and especially as a result of the introduction of the Welfare State, it is now considered to be part of the educational provision of the state. However, in more recent years its position has been threatened by the increasing emphasis on vocational education and training which, incidentally, also has a long history in civil society. Hence, the various forms of the education of adults have now become an element in government policy, which means that it has become increasingly important to develop a political understanding of the education of adults.

The idea of a politics of adult education has occurred frequently in the field of adult education, but its emphases have always come from a radical perspective rather than from that of political theory. Such an approach reflects the history of liberal adult education. This book is offered as an introduction to the study of the political theory of the education of adults. In the opening chapters the relationship between adult education and civil society is explored and, thereafter, theories of the state are examined. Policy and justice are the focus of the third chapter whilst the fourth looks at the way that the structures and content of adult education can be related to the bureaucratic state. Adult educators, in common with politicians, have tended to expound the benefits of democracy, although the term is rarely defined, and so the fifth chapter discusses the concept of democracy and shows that there are a variety of different forms with which the education of adults might be related. The idea of citizenship is also examined in this chapter, and this leads quite naturally into the discussion on human and citizenship rights in the sixth chapter, where it is suggested that the education of adults might be regarded as a citizenship right which is being lost to all citizens at the present time as a result of current government policies. The seventh chapter examines the idea of interests and relates these to the more popular educational term of needs. This chapter also examines community education and sees radical adult education as a social movement. Chapter eight focuses upon the relationship between liberal adult education and a civilised society, and suggests that its provision is one of the symbols that a society is moving on the long the journey towards creating a civilised society. In this chapter the instrumental rationality of the market is also examined and contrasted to value rationality. The final chapter illustrates the existence of utopian thought in radical adult education and raises questions about the education of desire.

This book has been a long time in the writing although some of its ideas have already been worked out at various conferences and published elsewhere. However, the previous publications do not occur within the same framework as they do here. I am listing these publications so that readers will be aware of the background of this work. In addition, I wish to record my appreciation to colleagues who have invited me to contribute to this debate.

Joachim Knoll invited me to the twentieth anniversary conference of the *International Yearbook of Adult Education* and the paper which I presented was subsequently published as 'Adult education and social-political policy' in the *International Yearbook of Adult Education*, 1989.

Franz Pöggeler invited me to speak at a conference at the University of Aachen and that paper was published as 'Adult learning, education and democracy' in *The State and Adult Education* which he edited (Peter Lang, Frankfurt, 1990).

Roger Fieldhouse invited me to contribute to another conference on the state at the University of Exeter and that paper was published in *The International Journal of University Adult Education* (November 1990) as 'Theories of the state and adult education'.

Franz Pöggeler and Kalmon Yaron organised a conference at the University of Jerusalem on crises and adult education, the papers of which were published in a book entitled *Adult Education in Crisis Situations* which they edited (The Magnes Press, Hebrew University of Jerusalem, 1991), in which my paper 'After the crisis – the promise of adult education' appeared.

Finally, Matti Parjanen asked me to speak at a conference at the University of Tampere on 'Legitimation in adult education' and that paper was published in the proceedings as 'Certification and the bureaucratic state'.

Not only do I wish to express my appreciation to these colleagues, I am also more than grateful to Bob Brownhill, of the University of Surrey, who read the first six chapters of this book and commented on them. This work has benefited greatly both from his critical comments and to the exposure of colleagues in the conferences mentioned above. At the same time, its weaknesses can only be attributed to me.

This book has also benefited from the constant understanding of my family who have supported me when I have been away speaking at conferences and who have continued to do so in the hours that I have spent 'away' in my study writing. To them, I am truly grateful.

Peter Jarvis
Guildford

1

THE EDUCATION OF ADULTS AND CIVIL SOCIETY

Throughout much of its history the education of adults has been located within civil society, although in many countries in the twentieth century it has become a matter of state policy. In some countries aspects of state involvement in vocational education was very early. For instance, in Britain, the state was involved in vocational education from the Elizabethan period, when there was enacted a Statute of Apprentices and Artificers, but later the state was to disengage from its educational involvement (P. Keane, 1988). In a few countries liberal adult education became a matter of state concern earlier than the twentieth century; for instance this occurred in Denmark as early as 1812. But in England, despite its early involvement in vocational education, the nineteenth century was largely one of *laissez faire* in accordance with the policies advocated by Adam Smith, among others.

That the education of adults has now become a matter of state policy is one of the reasons for this study. But before the major issues to be discussed in this book can be explored, it is necessary to clarify the concepts: the education of adults, civil society and the state. This constitutes the focus of the first two chapters; the first part of this one examines both the education of adults and civil society and the second part demonstrates that traditionally the education of adults has occurred in civil society although the state has frequently sought to control it. It will also be argued that the form of that education has altered relative to the changes that have occurred in civil society. The second chapter examines a variety of ways of interpreting the concept of state and the complex inter-relationship between state and civil society – thus setting the scene for the remainder of the book.

THE EDUCATION OF ADULTS

To most the idea of the education of adults is a self-evident concept but, unfortunately, throughout the history of its study the definitional problems have constituted a major obstacle because some scholars have sought to be more exclusive than others. Some, for instance, have wanted to define it within the framework of liberal-humanism and exclude all forms of training (Paterson, 1979), while others have confused education and learning so that they have regarded all forms of learning as educational (Long, 1983, Peterson *et al.*, 1980). More recently several scholars have focused on forms of learning, such as preconscious and incidental learning, that have to be excluded from almost any definition of education (see Jarvis, 1987; Marsick and Watkins, 1990 *inter alia*) so that it is essential from the outset to recognise that whilst there is considerable overlap between the two concepts of education and learning, they are not quite the same.

For the purposes of this study, education is regarded as the institutionalisation of learning. Institutionalisation is a sociological concept which refers to the process whereby specific social processes are habitualised and then treated as repetitive and continuing social phenomena which have become social institutions. Such processes are often regarded as unalterable, they become ritualised, and then objectified. Some forms of learning which occur regularly in some locations do become institutionalised and these are regarded here as education. At the same time it must be recognised that the distinction between the two is not clear-cut, and so there are still certain situations where institutionalised learning might not be treated as education – such as the coffee houses of the seventeenth and eighteenth centuries in England and the *salons* in France (Kelly, 1970: 54–9; Habermas, 1989: 32 *inter alia*) – which were places both of discussion and occasionally of debate and lecture. They provided opportunities for learning, some of which might also be classified as educational. Despite this difficulty, for the purpose of this study, education is treated as the institutionalised process of learning. This institution has become a social phenomenon which has been incorporated in the structures of society.

Of course learning does not take place only in formal situations – indeed, the situation may be formal, non-formal or informal, but it is open to question if learning should be classifed as education when it occurs in informal situations. Coombs and Ahmed (1974: 8) suggest that formal education is 'the highly institutionalised, chronological graded and hierarchically structured "education system", spanning lower primary school and the upper reaches of the university'. While the precise detail that they spell out is disputable, and certain forms of education of adults might also be included here such as initial professional education, their intention is clear – formal education is that social sector which has been fully incorporated into the society and socially defined as education. It will later be argued that this has become an instrument of state, or at least it has the potential of so being since it is the recipient of state policy and funding. Non-formal education, according to Coombs and Ahmed (1974: 8), is 'any organized, systematic, educational activity carried on outside the framework of the formal system to provide selected types of learning to particular subgroups in the population, adults as well as children'. It will be suggested later that some of these forms of education can also be state controlled. Indeed there are departments of non-formal education in some Third World state ministries controlling education, but much of the non-formal education is located and controlled by agencies in civil society.

At this stage the concept of 'educational' needs some clarification, since it might be asked if the knowledge being transmitted has to be worthwhile, and if so – worthwhile to whom (Peters 1966)? This becomes significant if, for example, it is argued whether a documentary on television is an educational programme or an advertising feature, even if it is produced by a political party explaining its intended political agenda to potential supporters amongst the public. At what point then does the transmission of information cease to be educational? This question is even more important when, for instance, the programme is not about a multi-national company's products but an attempt to warn people about AIDS, and so on. Certainly, the latter might be regarded as educational by many proponents, although it might just as realistically be argued that the state is using a non-educational approach (indoctrination) to transmit worthwhile knowledge in order to achieve beneficial social ends. Whether the process is educational or indoctrinational may be irrelevant to the recipients of the information, but it does raise both conceptual and methodological questions if it is to be regarded as educational.

In order to overcome some of these questions, it is suggested that if the motive for the programmes and the method of their presentation is humanistic, then they might be regarded as educational, so that education is treated here as 'any planned series of incidents, having a humanistic basis, directed towards the participant(s) learning and understanding' (Jarvis, 1983: 5). This approach helps solve some of these dilemmas, and the rationale for the definition has been more fully worked out in that earlier study. Even so, it must be recognised that this is an individual and personal operational definition, and that anybody can provide a definition for a teaching and learning process and call it educational.

However, the process of seeking to define education is revealing for two major reasons: first it demonstrates most clearly that the educational process is not one which has a universally agreed or unchanging definition. It is both a social institution and a process, the nature of the latter being open to debate. It follows from this, therefore, that defining the educational process is not only the prerogative of academics – it might also be the right of others, such as politicians! Indeed, this is an important point with which to commence this study, for if specific people control the media and also the funding for the process, it is possible for them to present their own understanding of education widely and influentially so that their perceptions become taken for granted and assumed to be the 'correct' definition. Take, for instance, the way that the hypothetical people in the street, if asked to define education, might immediately begin to define it in terms of children being taught, since initial education has become associated with education *per se* in their minds. Take also the illustration used above about AIDS education; educationalists might regard the process as indoctrinational whereas politicians might see it as educational. Any definition of education, therefore, reflects the ideological and ethical preconceptions of the definer or communicator of the definition, rather than an absolute and unchanging reality.

Having made this point, it is still necessary to recognise that definitions do reflect social processes. Additionally, when such definitions appear either jargon-ridden or pedantic, they may be seeking to describe precisely an understanding of social reality, with the more precise definition seeking to convey a very accurate meaning. Consequently definitions of phenomena are frequently sub-divided in order to communicate even more precise understanding, such as the distinction between formal and non-formal education. In addition, Coombs and Ahmed (1974: 8) regard informal education as that:

> lifelong process by which every person acquires and accumulates knowledge, skills, attitudes and insights from daily experiences and exposure to the environment.... Generally, informal education is unorganized and often unsystematic: yet it

4

accounts for the great bulk of any person's total lifetime learning.

In the main, therefore, their concept of informal education is actually learning in informal and incidental settings and, as such, it is not regarded here as a necessary part of the educational process. For this reason, education is treated here as those learning processes which occur within the formal or non-formal structures of society. This does not mean, however, that the teaching method or style utilised during the educational process might not be informal – the point being made here is that both formal and non-formal refer to the social structures within which the process occurs.

The distinction, made above, between the practice and the social institution of education must be discussed here. That sector of society, called education, and controlled by the relevant government ministry is often separate from those locations where the education of adults is practised, which are not necessarily in the sector of society regarded as education. For instance, nurse education is controlled by the Department of Health through the nursing profession, and so on. This distinction is important, since it can be seen that some of these continuing and professional educational forms are also state in-fluenced or controlled, but by ministries other than the Department of Education.

The concept of 'adulthood' has also been debated by adult educa-tors with some placing their emphases upon the age, and others on the maturity of the learner. Such a debate, however, is incidental to the purpose of this study and so it is unnecessary to consider it further here. The focus in this section is upon the social structures of society and, therefore, the formal school system is omitted, irrespective of the age when the student leaves it, whether it be twelve or 20 years! The structural problem, however, lies with further and higher education because there is an increasing number of adults returning to education and entering these sectors in order to study for a qualification, a first degree, a higher degree or even in continuing professional education, despite the fact that these sectors have traditionally catered for young adults only. The only common factor in these cases may be that there has been some break in time between their initial education and their continuing education, which might vary from a few weeks to many years. In other words, initial education is an uninterrupted period of formal education, which begins in childhood and continues uninterrupted for a variable number of years, until either the official school leaving age or until the completion of further or higher education.

Hence for the purpose of this study the education of adults is regarded as all institutionalised forms of learning that occur after the end of initial education, and these can occur both within formal and non-formal sectors of society. However, the extent to which they might now be regarded as part of civil society is much more debatable.

THE CONCEPT OF CIVIL SOCIETY

It is almost impossible to separate civil society from the state – there are those utopian socialist thinkers who look forward to a stateless utopia – a civil society without government because humankind is sufficiently mature to live without the intervention of a governing body and there are others, mostly more conservative, who look back to a time of the 'noble savage' who also needed no government. Both, in their different ways, are utopian and reference will be made to utopian thought in the final chapter of this book. However, it is important to recognise that the inter-relationship between state and civil society is extremely complex. It is discussed here in order to illustrate something of the history of the education of adults in society. In fact, J. Keane (1988: 14) defines civil society in terms of non-state activity:

civil society can be conceived as an aggregate of institutions whose members are engaged primarily in a complex of non-state activities – economic and cultural production, household life and voluntary associations – and who in this way preserve and transform their identity by exercising all sorts of pressures or controls on state institutions.

On the same page, Keane goes on to make the point that civil society has a certain potential to: 'become a non-state sphere comprising a plurality of public spheres – productive units, households, voluntary organizations and community-based services – which are legally guaranteed and self-organizing.' In one sense Keane is trying to illustrate this complex relationship of state and civil society historically – for some it is something that is backward looking but, in the second quotation, it is something which can look forward to the type of society envisaged by Robert Owen, and others of his utopian socialist persuasion. But the fact that Keane has to define the one in terms of the other indicates that there is no easy demarcation between them. Civic society, however, has not remained a static phenomenon over time, and Habermas (1989) has superbly illustrated the way that it has changed in his discussion on the public sphere. In the first instance (1989: 2) he relates public with state – 'The state is the "public authority"' since its task is to promote the common welfare of its members, but then (p.30) he goes on to show how, in the eighteenth century, the public sphere sub-divided and part of it became the civil state:

> The line between state and society.... divided the public sphere from the private realm. The public sphere was co-extensive with public authority, and we consider the court part of that. Included in the private realm was the 'authentic public sphere', for it was a public sphere constituted by private people. Within the realm that was the preserve of private people we therefore distinguish again between private and public spheres. The private sphere comprised civil society in the narrower sense.

Habermas then discusses the function of public opinion in putting the state in touch with the needs of society. For him, at this time, civil society was the sphere of private autonomy, of the free market of exchange and of civil law to regulate it. Habermas clearly recognises that the public sphere constituted by private people is not one in which all people participate equally, and so public opinion is not, in fact, the opinion of everybody – but of a bourgeois elite rather than the population.

It was the political discussions held amongst the elite which created the public place of civil society – the property owning people were regarded as those who could and should engage in critical public debate so that an ordered society might evolve; it was to be a freely competing society of 'property owning private people emancipated from domination and insulated from the intrusions of power' (Habermas, 1989: 111). However, the clash of interests meant that the civil society was not a rationally ordered society but a sphere in which interests clashed and competed so that disorder and instability were always possible. Hence, it had to be held together through political force – a state apparatus. Consequently, it later became necessary to consider the rights of people, as individuals and as citizens.

Later in his examination of the development of civil society, Habermas documents two major changes: the first is the fact that the state was forced to intervene into the affairs of civil society, a phenomenon that continued from that period through to the 1960s and

7

1970s when there were socialist welfare states in many parts of the world. The reaction to this occurred in the late 1970s and 1980s, after Habermas' study had been published in Germany, when the political slogans included, amongst others, that of 'rolling back the state'. This has resulted in the dominance of the competitive market and the influence of management and consultancy companies who are accountable to nobody but the institutions who employ them. This point will be discussed more fully later in the book, but its significance lies in the fact that there has also been a virtual disappearance of structural public places in civil society where issues of a democratic nature can be debated. Consequently, the large privately owned and multi-national corporations now have a virtual monopoly of power in the civil sector of society and, unless there is state intervention, they control the market by sheer financial power, which undermines the processes of democracy.

A major correlate of this decline of structural public space lies in the fact that civil society has changed from a culture-participating to a culture-consuming society during this period. Habermas (1989: 160) writes: 'The public sphere in the world of letters was replaced by the pseudo-public or sham-private world of culture consumption.' This resulted in the public sphere apparently becoming apolitical – no discussions of a political or religious nature allowed! – and even where the political debate has been encountered, it has been within the context of a televised discussion, or the presentation of the news – with contributions and comments by the experts. It has become part of the public entertainments industry and even as this book is being written there has been discussion in the United Kingdom about the fact that the television news should become a profit-making industry! Moreover, it is now commonplace to hear the television newscaster refer to an item of news as a 'story', indicating the way in which news is transformed for the sake of public consumption. Habermas (1989: 201) summarises this position succinctly: 'The public sphere becomes the court *before* whose public prestige can be displayed – rather than *in* which public critical debate is carried on.' (Italics in original.) This can be seen perhaps most clearly when ministers of state appear on television chat shows in which the presenter asks a few friendly questions, but rarely are they subjected to critical debate. Even parliamentary proceedings are presented to the public on television so that the people can view the outworkings of democracy! But perhaps it is also becoming increasingly obvious that this tends to be critical debate for but little of the time, and for much of the remainder the

8

debate is merely a presentation of rival political parties' pre-determined policy positions which have been decided by the respective party elites elsewhere. This is no more than a representation of democracy, performed for public consumption. Moreover, the hegemonic influence of those who control large industrial and commercial companies in civil society still needs to be fully documented!

Significantly enough, even the interest groups have to engage in activities that will get them noticed in television and radio reports, their activities are less frequently those of engaging in public critical debate, but much more in seeking to present their case, or at least in undertaking activities that will get them news space in the media – to be consumed by the public. Thus the outworkings of democracy have become something to be consumed rather than to be participated in; even public opinion is tested by opinion poll rather than by the active involvement of the public in the democratic process.

Civil society remains, but changed. Its potential still remains, but because of the way in which the state has been 'rolled back' it has become increasingly dominated by the market, not the market of a century ago, but by a new market controlled by multi-national companies and large management consultancies, and this is currently presented as a free market. But the inequalities which are currently prevalent in such a civil society have become more self-evident, which perhaps calls for a different relationship with the state, one which is in accord with the arguments of fairness and justice, advocated by scholars such as Rawls (1971), and this is more fully discussed in the eighth chapter. At the same time those who dominate civil society today have access to the media, present their cases in order to influence public opinion, or at least try to ensure that there is now little or no critical debate about their position, so that the public is kept relatively quiet. If, however, the media ask too many searching questions then politicians claim that it is biased and that its freedoms need to be curtailed.

It is into this type of background that the political debate about the education of adults needs to be located, and so the final part of this opening chapter endeavours to trace briefly the history of the education of adults in relation to civil society.

THE HISTORY OF THE EDUCATION OF ADULTS AND CIVIL SOCIETY

Whilst most educationalists, and indeed most people, regard education as self-evidently good, clearly this is not the way that everyone sees it, and, as a consequence, the education of adults has not necessarily enjoyed a smooth historical development. Indeed, it reflects many of the struggles that have occurred throughout the history of civil society. However, the demarcation between state and civil society is a relatively late phenomenon, and the education of adults emerged long before the nation state. At the same time much of the very earliest education of adults revolved around the politics of the city state; for instance in places like Athens. Concurrent with the rise in influence of the city states in Greece, there was a considerable amount of education of adults in societies such as among the Israelites, where the prophets of the Old Testament actively sought to teach the people about a variety of subjects such as social justice, individual responsibility and the meaning of life. Non-formal education of adults, therefore, began very early in the history of society. Since there was no nation state these expositions were either sponsored or conducted by the power elite (often of the religious institutions) or were of a more radical nature in which the elite were criticised and the criticism frequently assumed a religious form.

Adult education in England, according to Kelly (1970) also began with the religious institutions. In the opening chapter of his history of adult education in Britain he states:

> Historically the earliest motive for adult education was religious, and if we begin our story with the Anglo-Saxon settlement of Britain we may say that the first recorded adult educators were missionaries who came from Ireland or the Continent to convert the heathen inhabitants of this island to Christianity.
>
> (Kelly, 1970: 1)

Before the creation of the state in Britain, non-formal education of adults had been practised and established for years. Indeed, it was the Christian church in Britain that perpetuated the early education of adults and even established the first libraries where books could be read. With the Lollards, non-conformist and more radical approaches to education began. Wider perspectives on the education of adults only really commenced with the Reformation, the printing press, the growth of science and technology, etc. During this period, adult literacy, in order to read the bible also became more important because of the emphasis that Puritans and other non-conformist religious groups placed upon the bible as the word of God. Kelly (1970: 21) claims that the first formal adult education that he has discovered was

10

of Puritan ministers teaching adults to read. In the same manner, self-directed learning groups emerged in order to study the bible, some of these groups were to become the forerunners to study circles (Oliver, 1987), although these were not to become very popular until Wesley's class meetings were held during the period of the growth of Methodism in the eighteenth century.

The seventeenth century saw the growth of the coffee houses in Britain and by the start of the eighteenth-century London alone had 3,000 coffee houses; originally temperance establishments, these houses provided a forum for discussion under strict rules:

> Any man who paid his penny, whatever his rank, knight or commoner, bishop or curate, rich merchant or poor apprentice, was expected to take the first vacant seat, to expect civil conversation from his neighbour, and to participate in any discussion that might be going on. It would, of course, be unrealistic to suppose that the conversation was always at a high and serious level. Most of it must have been mere gossip, but a good deal of serious discussion obviously did take place on the political, religious, literary and scientific topics of the day, and some of the London coffee-houses were intellectual centres which brought together many of the best minds of the day.
>
> (Kelly, 1970: 54)

Coffee houses were public places in which people could congregate and participate in the intellectual debates of the day. They were places where public opinion could be created and moulded. Occasionally they were also places where more formal educational enterprises were embarked upon, with lectures and debates, and so on. One even had its own museum. Here then people, usually artisan and bourgeoisie, participated in the culture and the democratic processes in the public places of civil society but even here there were occasions when the state actually attempted to suppress the freedom of speech that existed in them.

Therefore, it was during this period that the power struggle between civil society and the state first became evident in the field of the education of adults. In the first instance the state and Church collaborated in the control of information that could be disseminated through the printed word. Opinions which were regarded as seditious or heretical were censored (Kelly, 1970: 61) and this was typified by the 1662 Printing Act which imposed censorship on books and newspapers, and strict regulations on the number of presses, printers and

11

booksellers. In addition, the law of seditious libel allowed the state to repress any written criticism of government. Only when the 1662 Law was allowed to fall into disuse was there a growth in newspapers and thus a greater freedom in the transmission of knowledge to the people. Thus it may be seen that at this time the state imposed strict control over certain elements of the education of adults in civil society, although it was in and through civil society that almost all the forms of educational innovation occurred.

With the emergence of science, many public lectures and classes were started but the size of the enrolment fee indicates that these catered for the bourgeoisie and artisans rather than the masses. Private clubs and societies were formed and a wide variety of subjects offered and later the mechanics institutes emerged with the purpose of disseminating scientific knowledge to working class people. The founders of the institutes had different motives for establishing them, some tended to regard them as organisations through which the working classes could gain sufficient knowledge to alleviate their poverty, others as a means of ensuring that the lower classes would learn to be more obedient to the laws and learn the rationality of the middle classes, whilst a few educators, such as Birkbeck, regarded them as agents of cultural change. Paradoxically, however, it was the Church and some members of the Tory party who opposed the growth of this secular education of adults in nineteenth-century Britain, frightened that an educated population would destroy the established order. The radicals, however, were generally very supportive of the adult education movement (P. Keane, 1988).

However, there was a tendency for the mechanics institutes to attract only a middle-class clientele. Education was being provided by an enlightened bourgeoisie for the mass of people, but the failure to attract them indicates the nature of the education that was being offered. The masses were expected to receive rather than participate, and to be passive recipients of the bourgeoisie's well-intentioned offering. At the same time, without some limited state support, even this voluntary movement would have faltered (P. Keane, 1988).

By contrast, a variety of working class movements were formed in nineteenth-century England, as Kelly (1970: 134f) notes:

> The various working class movements of the early nineteenth century, from the Hampden Clubs to the Chartists, were indeed shot through with educational idealism, and although our present knowledge of their activities is scrappy and inadequate,

enough is known to make it clear that their contribution to adult education was by no means negligible.

The Methodist movement, the co-operative movements, the workers' movements and the Chartists all had educational activities, some of which were regarded by the state and the employers as quite unacceptable. The aims of some of these movements might not seem too radical today; the London Working Men's Association had amongst its aims free circulation of thought, the education of the rising generation, freedom to meet and communicate ideas and the freedom to publish views in order to create a moral, reflecting public opinion. Nevertheless, some of the leading exponents of this approach to education were imprisoned, for example Thomas Cooper, a Chartist, was imprisoned for two years for seditious conspiracy.

Adult education became more institutionalised during the early part of the nineteenth century with the formation of adult schools. Once again the churches played a significant role in their foundation and continued to play a major role right into the twentieth century (Hall, 1985). Many other adult education movements began during the nineteenth- and early twentieth-centuries – the university extension service, Workers' Educational Association, and so on. None of these was started by the state, they were all civil movements. Indeed, the liberal thinkers of the period were most unhappy about the state being involved in education at all because they recognised some of the problems. In 1859, J. S. Mill (1962: 239f.) wrote about children's education:

> If the government would make up its mind to require every child a good education, it might save itself the trouble of providing one. It might leave to parents to obtain the education where and how they pleased, and content itself with helping to pay the school fees of the poorer classes of children, and defraying the entire school expenses of those who have no one else to pay for them. The objections which are urged with reason against State education do not apply to the enforcement of education by the State, but to the State's taking upon itself to direct that education; which is a totally different thing. That the whole or any large part of the education of the people should be in State hands, I go as far as any in deprecating.... A general State education is a mere contrivance for moulding people to be exactly like one another: and as the mould in which it casts them is that which pleases the predominant power in government,

whether this be a monarch, priesthood, an aristocracy, or the majority of the existing generation; in proportion as it is efficient and successful, it establishes a despotism over the mind....

Indeed, this has been the position held by many adult educators and so the concern has nearly always been to seek to establish adult education institutions free of state control. However, the history of adult education worldwide repeats the conflict depicted in the history of English adult education. Adult educators have had their institutions closed by the state whenever they have questioned its power base in society. A classic example of this was the Highlander Folk School in Tennessee, USA. Myles Horton and his school were involved in the civil rights campaign and as a result in 1962 the school was closed and the property confiscated by the state authorities. Horton, however, acquired new premises and registered it as the Highlander Research and Education Center and continued his work (Glen, 1988: 173). Additionally, Christian movements in South Africa, and elsewhere, involved in human rights and education have suffered at the hands of the state.

Paradoxically, the folk high schools in Denmark, which had been part of Horton's inspiration in the foundation of Highlander, were started in the nineteenth century to protect a national culture, since German political pressure and culture was threatening Danish culture. Underlying the foundation of the first school at Rødding in 1844 was the philosophy that the school was for:

peasants and burghers (so that they) can receive such knowledge and skills as can be of use and for pleasure, not so much with regard to an individual's particular occupation and profession as to his position as a son of the nation and a citizen of the state....
(Skovmand, 1983: 324)

Here then, adult education functioned in close relationship with the state to protect civil society and it was opposed to a more powerful neighbouring state. It does, however, depict a different relationship with the state to that demonstrated thus far in England in the nineteenth century and, significantly enough, into the twentieth century as well.

Traditionally adult education has been a civil movement, free to help educate the people to play their part in the emergence of a more democratic society, but frequently opposed by those who exercise power in society because they do not want the people to be knowledgeable enough to question their activities. Naturally, there have been exceptions amongst those who gain power and there are significant times in history where the state has been prepared to support the people.

However, by the start of the twentieth century the state had began to play a role in the education of adults in many societies, even to providing adult education classes. The London County Council, for instance, provided liberal adult education evening classes in 1906 (Kelly, 1970: 289) but support was not great throughout England for many years, with the growth of support only occurring with the foundation of the Welfare State after the Second World War.

CONCLUSION

It has been shown that the state has not automatically been supportive of adult education movements throughout the past few hundred years; indeed, in many instances it has sought to curtail such activities which have almost all started as enterprises in civil society. However, there have also been occasions when the state has needed adult education, some when it has used it, others when it has supported it and still others when it has merely tolerated it. Naturally, this has depended in some cases on the content being taught, in others on the historical situation and in others on the political complexion of the governing elite. Many of these will become more evident in the pages that follow but before this can be undertaken it is necessary to clarify some ideas about the nature of the state.

REFERENCES

Coombs, P.H. and Ahmed, M. (1974) *Attacking Rural Poverty*, Baltimore: The Johns Hopkins University Press.
Glen, J.M. (1988) *Highlander: No Ordinary School 1932–1962*, Lexington: University Press of Kentucky.
Habermas, J. (1989) *The Structural Transformation of the Public Sphere*, (trans. T. Burger, assisted by F. Lawrence), Cambridge: Polity Press.
Hall, W.A. (1985) *The Adult School Movement in the Twentieth Century*, Nottingham: Department of Adult Education, University of Nottingham.
Jarvis, P. (1983) *Professional Education* London, London: Croom Helm.
—— (1987) *Adult Learning in the Social Context*, London: Croom Helm.
Keane, J. (1988) *Democratic and Civil Society*, London: Verso.
Keane, P. (1988) 'The state, laissez-faire and the education of adults in Britain', *International Journal of Lifelong Education* 7(1).

Kelly, T. (1970) *A History of Adult Education in Great Britain*, Liverpool: Liverpool University Press (2nd edition).

Long, H.B. (1983) *Adult Learning*, New York: Cambridge University Press.

Marsick, V.J. and K. Watkins, (1990) *Informal and Incidental Learning in the Workplace*, London: Routledge.

Mill, J.S. (1859) On Liberty, in Warnock op. cit., pp. 126–250.

Oliver, L.P. (1987) *Study Circles*, Washington: Seven Locks Press.

Paterson, R.W.K. (1979) *Values, Education and the Adult*, London: Routledge and Kegan Paul.

Peterson, R.E. and Associates – edited version (1980) *Lifelong Learning in America*, San Francisco: Jossey Bass.

Peters, R.S. (1966) *Ethics and Education*, London: George Allen and Unwin.

Rawls, J. (1971) *A Theory of Justice*, Cambridge MA: Belknap Press of Harvard University Press.

Skovmand, R. (1983) 'Grundtvig and the Folk High School movement', in C. Thodberg and A.P. Thyssen (eds) *N.F.S. Grundtvig: Tradition and Renewal*, Copenhagen: Der Dansk Selskab.

Warnock, M. (1962) *Utilitarianism: John Stuart Mill*, London: Collins, The Fontana Library.

2

THEORIES OF THE STATE
AND ADULT EDUCATION

State and society are sometimes treated as synonymous concepts in analyses of adult education, although they are conceptually different as the argument in the previous chapter shows. Sociology of adult education has concentrated on the social element, as befits sociological analysis and has, where appropriate, introduced the concept of social power. This approach has been more prevalent amongst those adopting a more radical approach. With few exceptions, however, the state has not been the focus of attention, even when the study has been about the politics of adult education. (See, for instance, Freire, 1985; Evans, 1987; Griffin, 1987; Pöggeler, 1990.) Indeed, much of Freire's analysis is notable by the absence of the state as a variable throughout his work, despite its revolutionary perspective. Griffin's analysis of social policy and adult education comes closer to the approach adopted here, although the starting point for this analysis is with some of the theoretical concerns of political science rather than welfare policy. The first part of this chapter seeks to demonstrate why theorists have argued the state is a necessary phenomenon in modern society and then it examines the concept itself. Thereafter the analysis examines a number of the major theoretical and ideological perspectives about the state and begins to suggest ways in which they may be related to the education of adults.

THE NEED FOR THE STATE

One of the central discussions in political theory is the extent to which there is a need for the state. Some, such as anarchists, clearly do not believe in its necessity, whilst others obviously do. Marxists consider that it should wither away, the classless society emerging as it disappears, but only after the dictatorship of the proletariat. Statists, both

17

liberal and conservative, contend that there is a variety of reasons why the state needs to exist, such as the total chaos that would probably emerge if there were no state – Hobbes' (1968) celebrated war of all against all. Nozick (1974: 88–119) contends that the emergence of the state has occurred in order to ensure that individuals' rights are protected, but he suggests that this explanation for the monopoly of power exercised by this protective institution has occurred in an 'invisible hand' manner. In this he seeks to refute anachists' claims that the state can emerge without violating individual rights. Another reason commonly adduced is because the division of labour in society has created a situation of total diversity, so that the state is necessary in order to unite the whole. Hall and Ikenberry (1989: 170) also claim that '[e]volution's hidden message is that primitive peoples *need* the state' (italics in original). The paradoxical thing about the state is that the actual exercise of power necessary to unite the people is also the very process that divides them, since it creates a situation of rulers and ruled.

Adult-education literature has tended to concentrate on the processes of teaching and learning and to omit the political implications of the discussion, but Kemmis (1985: 139–64) even treats reflection as a potentially political process. Over recent years the idea that adult education should create critical thinkers (Myers, 1987; Brookfield, 1987 *inter alia*) and that it should empower individuals has become a dominant theme in American adult-education literature. Indeed, the whole theory of autonomous and self-directed learners has assumed a philosophical and political position, that all people are free to pursue their own interests in whatever manner they wish. There has been a great deal of theorising about adult learning, much of which is based upon an individualistic conception of the person in which little or no consideration about the person-in-society, let alone the person-in-a-state, has been given. Such an approach is a weak form of liberalism, conservative since it seeks to be apolitical, and over-simplistic because if every adult were to be a self-directed learner, every adult were to become a critical thinker, etc., then the stability of society might indeed be threatened. Indeed, it might need the Leviathan of the state, which Hobbes (1968) postulated, in order to create stability, let alone unity, out of diversity. Other thinkers, however, would advocate that it is this freedom that makes for a better society and this debate is picked up again in the final chapter when utopian thought is explored.

THE CONCEPT OF STATE

Thus it becomes necessary to explore the concept of the state before this analysis proceeds any further. For some the state is the social institution which claims the monopolistic legal right to employ force within a specified territory, for example Weber (1964: 156). However, this definition is too restricted because it limits the state to the exercise of legitimate force and obviously its functions are broader than this, relating in some way to civic society. Yet it points to a significant feature about the nature of the state for Marxists – that it is essentially a repressive institution, even in its reformist manifestations. It is also upon this very point of repressiveness that Marx and Engels (1967: 82) focus, when they view it in class terms:

> the bourgeoisie has at last, since the establishment of Modern Industry and of the world market, conquered for itself, in the modern representative State, exclusive political sway. The executive of the modern State is but a committee for managing the common affairs of the whole bourgeoisie.

While Marx and Engels might be correct in the main, A.J.P. Taylor (1967: 29) has pointed out that this is an over-statement because the state has a life of its own and has its own interests to sustain, so that it cannot totally repress one class or else it will unleash forces that will result in instability and ultimately in some form of revolution, a point to which further reference will be made below.

Political theorists generally have grasped the fact, however, 'that no state can sustain itself through brute force alone' (Hoffman, 1988: 73), at least not for ever, and so coercion must go hand-in-glove with consent. It is this element in the nature of the state that relates it to civil society and which is crucial also for educationalists, as will be argued throughout this book. Indeed, Marxists have highlighted the fact that state seeks to gain consent by repression, often through the control of the social, civic structures, rather than using blatant force. Althusser (1972: 251ff.) points to the fact that the state controls the ideological apparatus, as well as the repressive apparatus of force. He postulated that there were at least eight state ideological apparatuses: religion, education, the family, law, politics, trades unionism, media and culture. Through each of these people can be socialised, albeit sometimes unknowingly, into consenting to the ways of the state's ruling elite. While Althusser perhaps overstated his case, since it is possible that none of these operate in a mechanical manner, and that occasionally they may also produce activitists who work for change rather than conformity, as Gramsci recognised when he advocated a form of 'conservative schooling for radical politics' (Entwistle, 1979). Therefore, the ideological apparatuses are very significant for the survival of the state and have to be handled with great care. It is here that Gramsci's (Joll, 1977 *inter alia*) important concept of hegemony enters the debate. Indeed, it could be argued that those who control the state are in a strong position only when the ideological apparatuses function effectively and produce consent, but they are weak when they have to resort to the use of force and show that they are in control; the use of force is their last defence. Hence consent must be produced and while it might be produced coercively, it is better produced in a Machiavellian manner in order not to utilise the forces of coercion openly. Hence, the state should not appear coercive, but rather passive and even permissive if it is to function smoothly.

The significance of this conclusion is that if the state functions in a Machiavellian manner, then people might be misled about the nature of the state and, ultimately, develop a false consciousness about their own interests. This false consciousness is something that Marx highlighted, when he maintained that the bourgeoisie control the state apparatuses in their own selfish interests. However the concept of falseness is itself open to question and it will be explored in greater detail later. This approach to social analysis has also been a concern of critical theorists in more recent years, since they claim that the people might not always be aware of their own interests, and this is a concept to which further reference is made below.

The state, then, appears to be at least a necessary evil, without which there might be chaos, but with it there is social division and the possibility, even the probability, of considerable deception of the people by their rulers. Naturally there is a variety of theoretical positions falling between these two extremes. But the state is a controllable social institution and those who exercise power over it must gain, but not necessarily seek, the consent – even the apathetic consent – of the people in society if they are to survive in their elite capacity. Fundamental to the state, however, is some form of system of surveillance (Giddens, 1985) and, usually, a political system which is devised to legitimise the process of control. At the same time, the elite claim the right to exercise force over the people to ensure the survival and smooth functioning of society if they fail to gain that consent – which is a very strange paradox indeed! Indeed, the very existence of the state appears to be an implicit denial that the people exercise power which, in turn, suggests that actual, rather than representative, democracy might not be entirely possible.

From the above discussion it may be seen that any definition of the state must be broader than that which allows it only the legitimate control of force. There is considerable agreement among contemporary theorists about the main features of the modern state, and these are well summarised by Dunleavy and O'Leary (1987: 2) who suggest the following five points: it is separate from other institutions and constitutes a public sphere; it is supreme law maker and has control of force; its sovereignty extends to all individuals within a specified territory; its personnel are recruited and trained in a bureaucratic manner; it has the capacity to extract revenue from the people within its jurisdiction through taxation.

Thus it may be seen that the state comprises those institutions of a society which may be controlled by the governing elite and through which it exercises power over the population in a specific geographical territory. However, it will be clear from the complexity of the above discussion that while there is some agreement about how the state is defined conceptually, there is no single understanding about the way that its power should be exercised over that territory. Perceptions about this differ according to the different political traditions and there is not total agreement about these: Nisbet (1986), for instance, claims that conservativism, liberalism and socialism are central ideological orientations; Hall and Ikenberry (1989) suggest liberalism, Marxism and realism; Coates (1990) liberalism, Marxism, social reformism and conservatism. Elsewhere, Jarvis (1985: 12) referred to the four major ideologies of conservatism, liberalism, reformism and radicalism. Even so, few of these grand political traditions, however they are specified, actually occur in 'pure' form in political reality, and political theorists, such as Dunleavy and O'Leary (1987) and King (1986), have endeavoured to highlight these various shades of political opinion.

RECENT IDEOLOGIES AND THE STATE

From the above discussion it is clear that there are a variety of ideologies that require discussion in this section in order to see how adult education may be related to them. Many volumes have been written about these from Plato and Aristotle to the present day. This brief section does no more than summarise some of the main ideas that might be incorporated into the four grand traditions mentioned

21

by Jarvis (1985) and, for the sake of convenience, they will be discussed in reverse order.

Radicalism

Radicalism has, over the years, assumed many forms and not all of them might be described as left wing. Indeed, Margaret Thatcher adopted the term to describe some of her policies in the United Kingdom during the 1980s. Indeed, such a claim might well be justified in as much as some theorists of the New Right have certainly espoused perspectives that broke with traditional Toryism. However, Margaret Thatcher's use of the term was probably more political in nature, seeking to refine the language of her opponents for her own purposes. In the normal sense, the radical tradition is a long and honoured political position which has assumed what might be called a left of centre location in the political spectrum. Amongst its manifestations have been certain forms of socialism, anarchism, utopianism, Marxism and so on.

Anarchists hold that there is no need for a state or the control that it exercises. They believe that humankind is mature enough to live in harmony without rulers and, consequently, with no state – it has no reference to the Hobbesian or journalistic conception of chaos that is often coupled with it. This is an idealistic position and one to which humankind might aspire but which it has certainly not attained, although at different times in history anarchistic experiments have been attempted, without a great deal of success. Indeed, humankind does not appear to be mature enough to sustain such an ideal type of society.

Marxism is closer to the anarchist end of the spectrum and a manifestation of radicalism. For the Marxist, the state is an evil phenomenon that is controlled by the bourgeoisie in their own interests, but after the revolution it will gradually disappear as humankind matures sufficiently to enable people to live together in a classless society. Until that time, however, the culture of the proletariat must prevail and, therefore, after the revolution, the dictatorship of the proletariat will ensure the transition to a stateless society. But the concept of the dictatorship of the proletariat is itself an indication that society needs a state. Although Marx was an idealist, and his view of the classless society demands as much maturity from human beings as does the pure anarchist state, he was also a realist about people. However, there is a sense in which his idea of the classless society, springing from his theory of social change, is slightly transcendental. The theory suggests that the thesis spawns its antithesis and out of the ensuing conflict synthesis occurs: the classless society will likewise produce an antithesis that results in conflict and in a further change in the structures of society. Hence, if his theories are consistent then the stateless society must either lie beyond the confines of time or be transient within the bounds of social change. In either case, it is not a realistic option, although it will be explored a little more thoroughly in the final chapter on utopianism. However, Marxism is sufficiently idealistic to provide a critical appraisal of political practices and of other theories of the state and these are increasingly common within adult education literature.

However, when a form of Marxism assumed political power the state became totalitarian under Stalin, whilst still calling itself the dictatorship of the proletariat. Totalitarianism will be discussed under the sub-heading of conservatism rather than here, although the fact that it can legitimately be discussed at both ends of the political spectrum indicates how these different viewpoints overlap with each other.

Social reformism

This is a tradition based upon state intervention and welfare and is the opposite to certain forms of liberalism, although it stems from the thought of prominent liberal thinkers, such as J.S. Mill. It finds its economic basis in the work of Keynes and T. H. Green, and its social formulation in the writings of Weber, Marshall and Tawney (see Elsey, 1987). Hall (1984: 9) makes the point that it is fundamentally pluralist since it separates economic power and political power and there is a sense in which it is a combination of capitalism and democracy.

Within this system social change can be engineered by those in power for the benefit of all the people without destroying the structures of the state. Individual human rights can be protected and the state should intervene to ensure that the people's basic needs and interests are met. Reforms should always be state initiated, but this is more democratic in its orientation than classical liberalism, although it is often regarded as an offshoot of liberalism. Hall (1984: 44) argues that the historical circumstances of the twentieth century led to the people gaining more power within the reformist state but the price paid was heavy; they were to remain subordinate to those who have

23

traditionally exercised power. Social reformism is to be found among Liberal Democrats, members of the Labour party and, perhaps even among those whom Margaret Thatcher called 'wets' in the Conservative party, although most of these were probably closer to the classical conservative tradition.

However, social reformism necessarily has to redistribute wealth and so it appears coercive to those who possess it and, additionally, it requires bureaucratic procedures to administer, which are themselves expensive, time-consuming and often inefficient. Consequently, such a state is bureaucratic and minimal statists can point to bureaucratic inefficiencies when they seek 'to roll back the state'.

Liberalism

Liberalism is an earlier tradition but one which overlaps with social reformism. It owes a great deal in its origin to the work of J.S. Mill. This tradition is based on the significance of the individual and the individual's rights and responsibilities. The state should not interfere with the basic rights and their protection is among its basic functions. Where there is a conflict of interests, the state's responsibilities are to arbitrate between them, to be reactive rather than proactive. Hence, the emergence of the concept of the minimum state; a state that protects the individual without interfering with individual rights. This does not imply that the state need necessarily be democratic. On the contrary, it may need to be authoritarian on occasions in order to ensure that those rights are protected. Gray (1986: 76–7) points out that the weakness of the minimum state theory is that the only way that it can raise the revenue to exercise its functions is through coercive taxation, which is contrary to the basic tenets of liberal minimum state. It will be recalled, however, that this was the fifth trait of the state specified in the earlier discussion and, indeed, it is possible to raise some taxation with the agreement of the people so that Gray's claim may be a little too sweeping.

That reformism and liberalism overlapped in the past century is perhaps best seen in their relation to pluralism. Classical liberals regarded society as a collection of individuals having rights. Within it the state only functions to protect life, limb and property whilst in all else the individuals are free to act legally as they wish (Mann, 1983; Gray, 1986). However, society has changed since the nineteenth century and individuals have apparently become less significant than parties and organisations (Weber, 1971), so that a classical pluralism

24

emerged in the 1960s in which the state was regarded as neutral although it had to arbitrate between the political and economic power bases within society. The state only intervened in response to the pressures of the plurality of social institutions and also in response to pressure exerted by interest groups formed for that specific purpose, and it was the prerogative of any individual to form such a group to agitate in society. Having such rights ensured that democracy apparently existed and that the people were free to act within it. However, in the United Kingdom, during this period there was a reformist government which tended to intervene in the affairs of the people more than some previous governments and this resulted in considerable social change and redistribution of resources during its period in office.

Conservatism

This owes its origins in England to Edmund Burke's reaction to the French Revolution and to the tremendous changes happening in England at the same time – of both a religious and industrial nature. This brief summary relies heavily on Nisbet's (1986) study of conservatism. In this tradition, the state is there to protect the traditions of the past, since the present is not totally free; this is a point to which further reference will be made in the discussion about the relationship of conservatism with the education of adults. However, the state's protective role should be exercised prudently, so that it does not transgress the established rights and autonomies of the main classes in society, which includes their freedom and their possession of private property. However, conservatism has always recognised that individual freedom is conditional on the needs of the state, so that even that freedom has had to be moderated and controlled. Therefore, the state has to protect and delegate but it should not try to create a society in which everybody is equal, since that is not in the natural order of things. At the same time conservatives have rarely opposed state action, since the state has the right to act to protect those in need and the people should respond positively to the actions of the state.

During the past quarter of a century the New Right, which while calling itself conservative is in some ways closer to the liberal tradition, has emerged and its appearance may be traced in the United Kingdom as a reaction to the problems of social reformism and pluralism. Classical pluralism faced a number of problems during the early 1970s because of the slowing down of economic growth and the rise in social unrest. This led to a feeling that some forms of unorganised social protest was not in the best interests of the people and that it was necessary for the state to have a professionalised decision-making process that provided 'a substitute for external political controls in many areas of state activity where the conventional pluralist emphasis on party politics and interest groups would [have been].... inappropriate' (Dunleavy, 1981: 205) Because society was so complex this neo-pluralist argument was plausible with the state being seen to be active in the affairs of people, providing the expert and the professional to act in the nation's best interests. A certain credibility was attached to this position since the government of the day had a reformist stance. Additionally, the state was seen to be active in debates with the elites of each segment of society – it became a pluralism of elites but it was one in which for the most part consensus was achieved and the state was seen to appear to be open and reasonably democratic (Mills, 1959).

However, this form of ideology of the state was not to last long and in the late 1970s liberal anti-pluralism came to the fore, a natural successor in the process of social change from the 1960s. In this approach, there was a return to classical liberalism in curtailing the activities of the state, even if only from intervening in the activities of the elites. The major change, however, was in the methodological rationale employed to justify its apparently restricted activities: the incorporation of the theories of classical monetarist economics and the workings of the market provided a new rationale for not intervening. Market forces are left to provide the apparent workings of democracy, since the market apparently functions on an exchange of equivalents and so the 'relations of production can do without a traditional authority legitimated from above' (Habermas, 1976: 22). This is in accord with the liberal view of the state but the view of the market is rather idealistic since it is an exchange in which the powerful nearly always win, but in which the weak can have a try, so that society appears to have a semblance of democracy! Now it is the elite of one segment of society, the economic sector, that prevails in society, and the government claims that it does not need pressure group activity because it has been given a mandate to govern the people as a result of elections. Hence, it must be left to govern in those areas where the market does not rule. However, one of the problems with this approach is that the market is so obviously biased in the interests of the powerful that the consensus achieved through the ideological apparatuses appears much more fragile, and people are more aware of the unequal biases in the affairs of the state. The very process of liberal anti-pluralism helps to destroy any false consciousness that the people might have and this might help unleash those forces of unrest or even revolution to which A.J.P. Taylor referred.

The final form of conservatism which will be looked at here is totalitarianism, most dictatorships also have to assume this form in order to survive. The totalitarian state is the one described by Bentham's *Panopticon* (see Bauman, 1988) or Huxley's *Brave New World*, in which those who rule totally control those who are ruled. Bentham's vision was of an institution in which the supervisors could see the inmates without ever being seen, and know them without ever being known. Likewise, the supervisors were viewed by the head-keeper whom they could never see nor know. The outcome, for Bentham, was total conformity and peace and calm but no individual freedom. Captured within this image is the idea of the bureaucratic state to which a chapter is devoted later in this book. But as Huxley showed, this state of affairs is unreal, since however sophisticated the social or genetic engineering, individualism will always somehow emerge and then the totalitarian social system will itself be under attack. Rulers have, at different times in history, tried to create such societies with little success, as the recent changes in Eastern Europe indicate.

These, then, are some of the major ideologies and their relationship to the state, and it is clear that during the past twenty-five years there has been rapid political change, with the activities of the state being at the centre of the theoretical debate. Little of this debate has been incorporated into adult education literature, with the exception of some of the Marxist arguments, and therefore the final sections of this chapter focus upon the implications of these different political theories for education in general and the education of adults in particular.

AFFINITIES BETWEEN ADULT EDUCATION AND POLITICAL IDEOLOGY

Neither adult education nor knowledge have intrinsic value nor meaning, but certain manifestations of both have affinities with the four traditions discussed above, and in this brief section some of these will be highlighted.

Conservatism, for instance, has affinities with the knowledge of the expert and with practical knowledge. It appears, in some ways, to espouse a form of anti-intellectualism. Nisbet (1986: 31–2) suggests:

> At stake in the conservative appeal to prejudice in human behaviour is a whole type of knowledge. It is the kind of knowledge that William James described as 'knowledge of' in contrast to 'knowledge about'. The first is the knowledge we acquire simply through experience, through direct exposure to life or at least major areas of life. Its essence is practicality. It becomes an integral part of our character because its origins lies in the process of habituation, or converting to generalized predisposition or 'instinct' the knowledge gained through experiment, conscious or unconscious, and ordinary trial and error.

Immediate and practical knowledge, then, are indicative of conservativism, so that perhaps it is no accident that many adult educators, including Usher (1989) and Jarvis (1991) *inter alia*, have begun to examine the idea of practice and practical knowledge. Indeed, the whole experiential learning movement is in accord with the underlying epistemology of conservatism even though it appears progressive. In contrast, expert knowledge once gained, need not be acquired experientially by others for it is a time-consuming way of learning, so that that knowledge can be taught and learned in a much more traditional and anti-progressive manner. Indeed, the knowledge that previous generations learned must be transmitted to the present generation and this can be undertaken through traditional teaching, since discovery learning techniques are not really necessary nor efficient in transmitting that which is already known. Abstract intellectualism does not find a great deal of favour with conservatives, so that the universities' traditional freedoms and functions have suffered greatly, especially in the manner that philosophy departments have become regarded as optional extras to the university scene.

Liberalism has had a long involvement with education and knowledge, with J.S. Mill writing a great deal about the value of learning if people are to play their role in democratic society. The emphasis that liberalism has placed upon the individual is such that almost anything that could enrich the life of the individual might be regarded as being valuable. Hence the idea that liberal adult education as being that form of education which exists for individual enrichment has become generally accepted for much of the twentieth century, and this will be more fully discussed later in this book. Indeed, it is in the interest of the people to have education, and individual interest is the language of liberalism. Some of these ideas emerged with the self-help movement in the classical liberal period (Stephens and Roderick, 1983).

Many of the ideas that have emerged in adult education in the United States since the middle of the twentieth century have also been liberal in their orientation. Andragogy and self-directed learning, critical thinking (as opposed to critical theory) and certain forms of self-discovery learning, and assertiveness training have all emphasised the individual and individual enrichment; all are based upon an individualistic liberal philosophy. It is, perhaps, the same emphasis on individualism that has resulted in American adult education being fundamentally psychological rather than sociological or philosophical in academic orientation.

As 'interest' is the language of liberalism, so 'need' is the language of social reformism. Social reformism is typified by state intervention and the welfare state, of which educational provision forms a part. It is perhaps significant that one of the most thorough analysis of the concept of 'need is to be found in the social welfare literature, where Bradshaw (1977) suggested that there are four fundamentally different forms of need: normative, felt, expressed and comparative. Coincidentally, Wiltshire (1973) rightly pointed out that the term 'need' begged a number of significant questions and although he did not pursue this line of argument, it would have been useful to have done so, since need is the language of social reformism but it is most commonly used by the providers of liberal adult education! Philosophically 'need' is a problematic concept since it has no empirical basis, so that it must be regarded as relative. It is, therefore, disputable on grounds of either its relativity or else upon the criteria decided upon to determine the standard below which a need might occur. Adult educators have never really discussed this in any depth, often having only an intuitive definition of the concept. Lawson (1975: 33–41) has provided perhaps the best analysis of need in the adult education literature and even he is forced to define it in terms of a deficiency that can be remedied by an educational process, which is problematic in the light of the fact that nobody is omniscient!

Griffin (1987: 18–28) has also located a great deal of adult education in liberal democracies in the framework of welfare provision, although it is removed from direct state provision since it is administered through the local government framework of society. One of the problems of regarding this form of education as a welfare provision, and many adult educators have tended to do this in order to justify what they do, is that it fails to analyse the social significance of the educational process and merely describes it by one of its social functions.

Radical adult education has often espoused Marxist, Christian or Christian-Marxist ideologies and these are epitomised by Freire and Horton (see Horton and Freire, 1990 for a good summary of their positions). However, much radical adult education tends to be reformist rather than revolutionary (Lovett, 1988 *inter alia*) since it exists to change society by peaceful not revolutionary means. Many radical adult educators have recently espoused critical theory and the work of such writers as Fromm and Habermas is beginning to appear more frequently in adult education literature. The language of radicalism includes such words as empowerment, although it should be noted that the idea of empowerment has been neutralised by its use by non-radicals. This is, indeed, a linguistic technique used as a political ploy.

Some of these forms of adult education are more egalitarian and their methods tend to reflect this approach. It is, however, quite significant that Giroux (1981: 63ff.) pointed out that with a few exceptions, such as Freire, radical educators in the United States had either become content-focused or strategy-based radicals rather than a combination of the two. By this he means that most educators either talked about radicalism but did not practise it or they used progressive, even radical, teaching techniques but they did not really espouse radicalism in the content of their teaching.

ADULT EDUCATION AND POLICY: AN INTRODUCTORY CASE STUDY OF THE UNITED KINGDOM

The state, by its very existence, must exercise control and this it does through force or through the manipulation of the social institutions, including education – often with the claim that it is in the national interest or to the public good. The extent to which these claims are valid might relate to the complexion of the political party which is apparently in control of the state apparatus.

It has been claimed elsewhere (Jarvis, 1985), however, that there are basically two forms of education: education from above and education of equals. But it is evident that since the state must control, by its very nature, the form of education that it will espouse will almost inevitably be one from above. This also points to one of the cruel paradoxes in the history of adult education for its pioneers worked altruistically, sometimes within a framework of the education of equals, for the common good, but they have also sought state recognition. But when they achieved this the outcome was the transformation of adult education into a form of state controlled education. Now the state may claim that it is still administered for the common good, a claim that is patently suspect in some situations where the institution has been manipulated for the benefit of the ruling party, although it might be claimed by some that on other occasions the elite have used education for the common good, even when it has been education from above.

However, Marxists clearly do not regard education as having been employed in such a benign manner but rather as the most significant of the state ideological apparatuses. Althusser (1972: 258), for instance, wrote:

> I believe that the ideological apparatus which has been installed in the *dominant* position in mature capitalist social formations as a result of a violent political and ideological class struggle against the old dominant ideological State apparatus, is the *educational ideological apparatus*.
>
> (Althusser's italics)

Indeed, Althusser points out that Lenin desperately sought to control the ideological apparatus, especially the educational one, in order to secure the transition of Russia to Lenin's brand of Marxism. Whatever the complexion of the ruling elite, it may be seen that education may be used in its interests.

However, one of the features of adult education has always been the liberal tradition, and this tradition has emphasised elements embodied in classical liberalism, such as the emphasis upon the individual as a rational human being able to learn and take the fruits of that learning and act in the world. Indeed, this was regarded as one of the main functions of education by John Stuart Mill – to provide an education so that adult human beings could play their full role in a democratic state, even if only through the election of their representatives! Since Mill's time, it is clear that individuals who have been through the liberal adult education system have been able to play a more significant role than merely voting for their representatives and that occasionally it has produced individuals who have been able to work to change the system, so that the critical appraisal of liberal adult education by Keddie (1980) is clearly only correct as far as she develops her argument. She suggests that adult education provision has always been a providers' model, that is adult education from above, rather than a genuine attempt to meet the needs of the people. In addition, since it contains an ideology of individualism it merely supports the cultural styles of the dominant classes in society and, therefore, reinforces its social and cultural structures. Whilst she is partially correct from the standpoint of her analysis, it may also be claimed that the middle class are more conformist in practice although individualistic in ideology and, that while the state still controls it, liberal adult education is still able to function so as to educate individuals who might be able to play a critical role in the activities of the state, although they are likely to be middle class and have an individualistic orientation. Hence, there are at least two ways of looking at liberal adult education – it contains the possibility of educating individuals who might play a full part in the affairs of state, but at the same time it acts as a hegemonic state apparatus because it appears to support the state structures implicitly in respect of those who reject the ideology of individualism.

However, Keddie wrote at the end of a period of pluralism when the State encouraged pressure groups to be active in society and adult education was able to play a part in this, as Newman (1979) showed so eloquently when he highlighted the way that adult education was able to respond to the demands of the minority groups. Since then the times have changed and the state has become liberal anti-pluralist and this has produced a new picture of the education of adults. In the first instance, its anti-pluralism no longer encourages pressure groups to act upon it and so the political element of adult education has become even less apparent. It has, therefore, automatically become more conservative.

Liberal anti-pluralism also claims that the state does not intervene in the affairs which rational human beings should be able to conduct without state intervention. However, by espousing the theory of monetarism in which the market prevails it has also enabled the large industrial and commercial companies to become even more dominant. This has had a major effect upon education of adults – it has been almost completely redefined as continuing education, which has become an apparently apolitical term although it was pointed out (Jarvis, 1983) that it would prevail over other terms because of its apparently non-political but actually conservative orientation.

Indeed, the government has been most active in the support of the development of continuing professional education through the creation of the Manpower Services Commission (which later became the Training Agency) and now has much of its power devolved to local TECS (Training and Enterprise Councils), and also through the PICKUP (Professional, Industrial and Commercial Updating) initiative. Manpower Services Commission courses were expressly forbidden to have political content and many were aimed at providing people with the opportunity of acquiring new skills and, where appropriate, finding work, even though there was very little available at that time! Gradually, continuing education has become more responsive to the demands of industry and commerce, educational standards are being determined to some extent by industry and even academic awards are becoming the prerogative of the powerful social institutions. However, the government also has intervened into society and funded ACCESS courses to higher education and the professions, but this is a reflection of the need to be seen to be providing opportunities for the underprivileged groups, initially ethnic minorities and later women, with a second chance. It is individualistic in orientation, but it may be interpreted as government support for the underprivileged groups who are clearly having little success in their endeavours to break out of their underprivileged position. If there had not been some obvious signs of political concern it might have resulted in even more social and political unrest among the minority groups. In addition, the government has funded REPLAN, an educational programme for unemployed adults, which may also be interpreted in a similar manner. Hence education is being used by the state in order to lower tension and such support will, no doubt, cease should the industrial and social situations change.

With the current curtailing of public funding to education and the encouragement to educational institutions to seek to liaise with industry in order to provide for its continuing education needs, it has encouraged the provision of a market economy in education where the strongest survive and the weakest fall, irrespective of the excellence of the education that they offer. More significantly, however, it has allowed industry to define educational needs, or at least allowed those who control industry to define education – both at school level and beyond – and made education subservient to it. Education has, therefore, been de-politicised and redefined so that it is now the handmaiden of industry and commerce – but it is still the apparatus of a government which can stand at the touchline and watch. It has achieved a form of consensus based upon the idea that education must be relevant to society's needs, even though these are now being partly defined by those who control industry and commerce.

Traditional liberal adult education has not been destroyed but it has also not received as much support from the state, although it has received some. It can be argued, however, that since it is a leisure pursuit for those who wish to spend their own time and money on it, it should not receive any state support – after all other leisure-time pursuits (such as bingo) do not. Once again the market forces must prevail and as such this form of education should not be highly subsidised, although the public outcry after the publication of the recent White Paper (1991) did cause the government to appear to back down on its more extreme proposals about self-financing liberal adult education. However, since it is still a liberal form of adult education it can still be encouraged within liberal anti-pluralism as something which is good and beneficial, since it can and does still produce educated people who are able to play a role in the wider society. But as a liberal form of education, it is open to all the individualistic class strictures that Keddie raised about it – it is still a part of the apparatus of the liberal anti-pluralist state – although the possibility of helping mostly middle class individuals to develop and play a more significant part in society still exists.

The state must control, that is at the heart of any understanding about the state. No state can allow an institution to exist that could undermine its credibility. It needs the consent of the people and so it would be problematic ever to regard institutionalised adult education in any other role than that of being subservient to the state. It might well be asked, therefore, whether there is any place for education of equals, any place for the type of adult education that has idealistic overtones? What of the work of educators like Paulo Freire? Do they have no place? Clearly this analysis has raised a number of quite fundamental questions about the place of adult education in the state and it is essential to pursue them rigorously later in this study.

CONCLUSION

Whatever the theory of the state, it must have the power to control and so institutionalised adult education will for the most part be a form of education from above, an instrument of state policy. Only in liberal and pluralist societies, where the state stands back and encourages individuals and interest groups to express their interests can an education from above be seen to work in part for the interests of the people rather than in those interests defined by the state. Indeed, it might only be in the social movements, such as feminism and the ecological movement, that adult education can genuinely be a process between equals, for in these instances it is an instrument of the interests of the members of the movement rather than the state. The educative function of pressure groups will be analysed in the seventh chapter of this book, but where adult education is non-formalised, it is more likely to function in response to the people's own defined interests. Once it becomes institutionalised, adult education exposes itself to become an instrument of state and this is almost an inevitability. But it is not inevitable that everybody who passes through the institutionalised system will be conformist and this is one of the dangers of education to the state – that it can never be completely controlled.

It is clear, therefore, that adult education is frequently an instrument of state policy and, therefore, the following chapter examines briefly some of the theories of social policy and relates these to the education of adults.

REFERENCES

Althusser, L. (1972) 'Ideology and ideological state apparatuses', in B. Cosin (ed.) *Education, Structure and Society*, Harmondsworth: Penguin Books in association with the Open University.

Anderson, J. and Ricci, M. (eds) (1990) *Society and Social Science*, Milton Keynes: Open University Press.

Bauman, Z. (1988) *Freedom*, Milton Keynes: Open University Press.

Bradshaw, J. (1977) 'The concept of social need', in M. Fitzgerald, (eds) *Welfare in Action*, London: Routledge and Kegan Paul in association with the Open University.

Brookfield, S. (1987) *Developing Critical Thinkers*, San Francisco: Jossey Bass.

Coates, (1990) 'Traditions of thoughts and the rise of the social sciences in the United Kingdom' in Anderson and Ricci, op. cit.

Dunleavy, P. (1981) 'Alternative theories of liberal democratic politics', in D. Potter *et al.* (eds) *Society and the Social Sciences*, Milton Keynes: Open University Press.

—— and O'Leary, (1987) *Theories of the State*, London: Macmillan.

Elsey, B. (1987) 'R.H. Tawney – Patron saint of adult education', in P. Jarvis (ed.) *Twentieth Century Thinkers in Adult Education*, London: Croom Helm.

Entwistle, H. (1979) *Antonio Gramsci: Conservative Schooling for Radical Politics*, London: Routledge and Kegan Paul.

Evans, B. (1987) *Radical Adult Education: A Political Critique*, London: Croom Helm.

Freire, P. (1985) *The Politics of Education*, Massachusetts, Bergin and Garvey.

Giddens, A. (1985) *The Nation-State and Violence*, Cambridge: Polity Press.

Giroux, H.A. (1981) *Ideology, Culture and the Process of Schooling*, London: Falmer Press.

Gray, J. (1986) *Liberalism*, Milton Keynes. Open University Press.

Griffin, C. (1987) *Adult Education as Social Policy*, London: Croom Helm.

Habermas, J. (1976) *Legitimation Crisis*, London: Heinemann.

Hall, J.A. and Ikenberry, G.J. (1989) *The State*, Milton Keynes: Open University Press.

Hall, S. (1984) 'The rise of the representative/interventionist state' in G. McLennan, D. Held and S. Hall (eds) *State and Society in Contemporary Britain*, Cambridge: Polity.

Hobbes, T. (1968 edn) *Leviathan*, Harmondsworth: Penguin.

Hoffman, J. (1988) *State, Power and Democracy*, Brighton: Wheatsheaf Books.

Horton, M. and Freire, P. (1990) *We Make the Road by Walking*, Philadelphia: Temple University Press.

Huxley, A. (1955) *Brave New World*, Harmondsworth: Penguin.

Jarvis, P. (1983) *Adult and Continuing Education: Theory and Practice*, London: Croom Helm.

—— (1985) *The Sociology of Adult and Continuing Education*, London: Croom Helm.

—— (1991) 'Learning practical knowledge', unpublished paper delivered to the *Professionals' Ways of Knowing Conference*, American Asociation of Adult and Continuing Education, Montreal.

Joll, J. (1977) *Gramsci*, Glasgow: Fontana.

Keddie, N. (1980) 'Adult education: an ideology of individualism', in J. Thompson (ed.) *Adult Education for a Change*, London: Hutchinson.

Kemmis, S. (1985) 'Action research and the politics of reflection', in D. Boud, R. Keogh and D. Walker (eds) *Reflection: Turning Experience into Learning*, London: Kogan Page.

King, (1986) *The State in Modern Society*, New Jersey: Chatham House.

Lawson, K. (1975) *Philosophical Concepts and Values in Adult Education*, Nottingham; University of Nottingham: Department of Adult Education.

Lovett, T. (ed.) (1988) *Radical Approaches to Adult Education: A Reader*, London: Routledge.

Mann, M. (1983) *Macmillan Student Encyclopedia of Sociology*, London: Macmillan.

Marx, K. and Engels, F. (1967) *Communist Manifesto*, Harmondsworth: Pelican.

Mills, C.W. (1959) *The Power Elite*, Oxford: Oxford University Press.

Myers, C. (1987) *Teaching Students to Think Critically*, San Francisco: Jossey Bass.

Newman, M. (1979) *The Poor Cousin*, London: George Allen and Unwin.

Nisbet, R. (1986) *Conservatism*, Milton Keynes: Open University Press.

Nozick, R. (1974) *Anarchy, State, and Utopia*, Oxford: Basil Blackwell.

Pöggeler, F. (ed.) (1990) *The State and Adult Education*, Frankfurt: Peter Lang.

Stephens, M.D. and Roderick, G.W. (eds) (1983) *Samuel Smiles and*

Nineteenth Century Self-Help in Education, Nottingham: University of Nottingham; Dept of Adult Education.

Taylor, A.J.P. (1967) Introduction to *Communist Manifesto*, in K. Marx and F. Engels *Communist Manifesto*, Harmondsworth: Pelican.

Usher, R. (1989) 'Locating adult education in the practical', in B. Bright (ed.) *Theory and Practice in the Study of Adult Education*, London: Routledge.

Weber, M. (1964) *The Theory of Social and Economic Organisations*, New York: The Free Press.

—— (1971) 'Class, status, party', in K. Thompson and J. Tunstall (eds) *Adult Education for a Change*, London: Hutchinson.

White Paper (1991) Further Education and Training for the 21st Century, London: HMSO.

Wiltshire, (1973) 'The concepts of learning and need in adult education' in *Studies in Adult Education*, 5(1) April.

3

STATE POLICY, JUSTICE AND ADULT EDUCATION

Whilst the minimal state theorists maintain that the state should play as little part as possible in civic society, it has become clear throughout this analysis that the state, by virtue of its nature, must control, even if it seeks to minimise the amount of its intervention. Thus it was shown in the last chapter how the state intervened in order to direct attention to vocational education but, by contrast, only to encourage the provision of liberal adult education. Thomas (1989: 105) has suggested that:

> It is possible to identify four major responses that all societies make in the management of learning. They can permit learning; in the sense that societies based on traditions of common law permit any activity that is not expressly forbidden; they can encourage the pursuit of certain learning objectives or outcomes; they can direct attention to specific outcomes, as is the case in all systems of education; or they can attempt to prevent or eliminate certain outcomes.

In many countries in the world a great deal of adult education is provided by voluntary associations, much of which is permitted or encouraged by the state, although there are times when their educational activities are frowned upon. Sometimes these activities are actually prohibited, especially when they appear subversive or threatening to those who control the state. This has certainly occurred in recent years with political, religious and workers' associations in countries with conservative or totalitarian governments and in countries that have been regarded by many commentators as being undemocratic.

Thomas suggests that the state encourages most forms of adult education and while he may be partly correct it is necessary to examine the political ideology of those who control the mechanisms of state to understand the process more thoroughly. It might have been argued for instance, in the introductory case study of recent events in the United Kingdom in the previous chapter, that the state encouraged liberal adult education, although it wished to withdraw financial support from it. But, it might then be asked, whether verbal encouragement without financial support is anything more than political rhetoric? Words are one thing, but the actions indicate that all the state is doing is permitting the existence of liberal adult education.

Thomas locates nearly all forms of formal education in the third category, i.e. the state requires certain forms of education to take place. However, he does not develop this to the extent of suggesting that the government sometimes requires all adults of a certain category to attend classes for their education, such as education for those who are unemployed. Minimal statists would regard this as excessive state activity and even one in which the state disregards the rights of the unemployed. Neither does Thomas extend his discussion to the situation where it might be argued that the state has the right to enforce adults to be educated in certain values and beliefs. However, it is argued by Cohen in Israel that:

> not only do we have the right, but as educators we have a **duty** to present to the adult learner the values, norms, and beliefs which we consider true and most appropriate for the time and place in which we live.
>
> (Emphasis in original)
> (Cohen, 1989: 37–8)

Cohen goes on to recognise that there are problems of indoctrination in claims such as this which he proceeds to deny, although he has a rather specific and perhaps limited conception of indoctrination as being only a teaching technique. Some theorists would include both aim and content within the context of indoctrinational practices (Hollins, 1964). But it must be recognised that any fine philosophical distinction between education and indoctrination is not necessarily going to concern those in power – formal education exists to serve society and the state and its functions can be defined politically, albeit within certain limits which may be relative to the historical circumstances. Significantly, however, Cohen does not examine the nature of the state in his chapter, although it might be argued that the historical and geographical position of Israel demands that the state be more interventionist in nature than it might be given different conditions.

However, the point of this introduction to the work of Thomas and Cohen is to illustrate that, for whatever reason, the education of adults must be regarded as an instrument of state policy, which makes it necessary to examine different approaches to policy. The remainder of this chapter falls into two parts; the first examines policy perspectives and the education of adults, and the final section relates this discussion to the ideas of social justice and legitimation.

SOCIAL POLICY MODELS AND THE EDUCATION OF ADULTS

While education has been extensively studied, its relationship to social policy has constituted only a very limited amount of that scholarship (ee Kreitlow and associates, 1981; Finch, 1984; Griffin, 1987; Dale, 1989). Kreitlow and his colleagues and Griffin concentrate on the education of adults, while Finch and Dale mainly examine the school system. Nevertheless the discussions of the latter two writers are as relevant to this discussion as that of the former.

Kreitlow and his colleagues examined a number of controversies in adult education, among them being the extent to which the state should be involved in adult education policy and whether adult education itself should be interventionist. In one of the essays in this book, Fellenz (1981) argues that the leadership role of adult education should remain with the educators, while, in another, Moore (1981: 213) makes the counter-claim that 'the federal government [is] the *only* agency that can assume a leadership role' (italics in original) in relation to the functions of adult and continuing education. Fellenz is adopting a typically American liberal position, while Moore adopts an interventionist argument. In none of the chapters in this volume, however, do theoretical models of policy occur explicitly, although there are significant issues raised which reflect the different political awareness of the authors. By contrast, Finch (1984) suggests that there are four different policy perspectives: welfare; as a service offered to to the recipients; social engineering; and meeting society's 'needs'. Griffin (1987) assumes that there are three approaches: market models; progressive-liberal-welfare models; and social control models. For the purpose of this section, Griffin's model of three different approaches is adapted by splitting his middle category into two, progressive liberal and welfare, since this relates closely to the previous discussion about the way in which the education might be viewed as an instrument of state.

Market models

Minimum state theorists have regarded the market as one of the major instruments for ensuring efficiency, a consequence of which is that the successful become more successful while the weak 'go to the wall'; as if success in the market is equivalent to quality! It is an approach that is consistent with both some forms of conservatism and traditional liberalism. It is also an approach that can and has been applied to education. In higher education in the United Kingdom, for instance, the idea of competing for limited funding has become an almost accepted norm – the assumption behind the government policy being that the competition and the market will produce both efficiency and quality in education, an assumption that appears to have little research justification in education.

However, there is a sense in which liberal adult education in the United Kingdom has always operated on something of a limited market approach as it has been mostly a voluntary leisure time activity. The normal practice has been for adult education providers to prepare a prospectus and offer the courses to the local community to see which would attract sufficient students for the course to be both educationally and financially viable. Until recently the market has been a virtual monopoly, with the local education authority adult educators preparing the prospectus and offering the courses, even selling them quite hard in all types of places, such as shopping centres (Martin, 1987), in order to increase the uptake of students, rather than to compete with any rivals in the market. However, recent years have seen the emergence of private adult education agencies in the local communities (Blamire, 1985) competing with the local adult education institutions for students, so that the market concept has become even more of a reality. Traditionally, the state has subsidised local authorities so that student fees could be kept at an artificially low level. This has made it harder for private agencies to compete with local authority institutions, but as the subsidies have been progressively withdrawn it has become easier for private agencies to compete. Hence, on the surface at least, the innovations that the Conservative government sought to introduce into the United Kingdom in the White Paper in the early 1990s by withdrawing financial support might be seen to be a rather insignificant change, although this was not the case for a variety of reasons – such as trying to draw artificial boundaries between vocational and non-vocational courses and confusing liberal and welfare adult education. The proposed policy changes were not popular and, in the first instance, caused a considerable reaction from adult educators.

Underlying the market model is the idea that education is a commodity, or at least educational courses or modules are commodities, which can be marketed. If the fee is not subsidised by the state, or the local government or some other agency, then it should be determined by the market on the economic principle of supply and demand. If courses cannot be produced at a fee that the market will bear, then the course should be withdrawn – irrespective of whether it is needed or not. It is the market that determines the outcome, not the usefulness or the quality of the educational offering, and if educational institutions are not sufficiently efficient then they should either change their approaches to education or close their doors.

As society has internationalised, this market approach has become even more prevalent, both with traditional modes of education and even more so with distance education. Educational institutions in the First World, seeking new clients for their educational commodities, are either sending out their representatives to Third World 'education fairs' in order to attract more students to come and study at their institutions, or they are offering a variety of distance education type courses throughout the world. Both of these approaches reflect the type of enterprise which is the hallmark of capitalism. The market has now been internationalised and educational institutions are now rival competitors, seeking to undercut the fees of, or to offer qualifications in shorter periods of study time or less amount of work than, their rivals in the market. The successful institutions rightly see a large potential market, whereas the unsuccessful ones might have to withdraw from the competition. This can, naturally, have dire consequences for the unsuccessful institutions in the market. But there is another, perhaps unforeseen, negative consequence of this marketing approach, for it puts at risk those struggling Third World educational institutions seeking to establish themselves in their own countries, increasingly against the competition of the distance education universities of the First World – similar consequences to those which have occurred in the past with other aspects of poor nations' economies!

Progressive liberalism models

This policy approach is closer to the beneficiary model which Finch suggested, and she uses adult education as its exemplar. Adult education might be regarded as being provided for individual benefit, to enrich the lives of those who wish to attend classes. It is about self-improvement, self-enrichment and, even, assertiveness training. However, some of these same reasons can be used to argue that elements of the traditional adult education provision are welfare rather than liberal, and this will be discussed in the following section. Indeed, the 1944 Education Act specified that further education should be promoted by the government and provided by local authorities for anybody able to 'profit by the facilities provided'. The Russell Report (1973: 5) in the United Kingdom adopted a similar approach:

> The needs being met by adult education are clear enough: creativity and craftsmanship in an age of mass production; enrichment in the home environment and of family activity; benefit from social mobility and enhanced opportunity; and voluntary association with others of like interest.
>
> (para. 15)

It is not only state provided adult education that can be analysed from this perspective, much of the education provided by the voluntary associations can also be understood from it. The Workers' Education Association, for instance, allowed 'its classes to work towards their own solution' (Field, 1990: 366), even from its earliest years. The Young Men's Christian Association, a large educational provider in the United States, also adopted a similar strategy. However, some supporters of the welfare provision of education for adults have been very concerned about the social mobility aspect – Mansbridge, for instance, did not wish the Workers' Educational Association to have examinable courses for this reason and the 150 Hour Programme in Italy has also adopted a similar strategy.

Welfare models

Much of the Russell Report also reflected a welfare model of adult education, which is reformist and interventionist. Stemming from the Welfare State, this approach assumed that because society, if left to itself, is neither equal nor just, it is the duty of the state to intervene and put to rights any structural injustices that occur. The growth of adult education provision in the 1960s in the United Kingdom can therefore be regarded, to some extent, as a development in welfare provision. However, welfare provision does need more justification than merely the assertion that it seeks to right injustices in society, especially when governments of more right-wing persuasions have been in power. Hence, there are a number of different interpretations of the welfare approach. Pinker (1971: 97–104) suggested two types:

> Residual Model – social welfare should focus selectively upon the residual and declining minority of needy groups but as the wealth of the nation increases these will require less assistance

> Institutional Model – since the market is unable to secure a just allocation of resources throughout society, there will always be a need for the social services.

The latter model is a recognition of the nature of market capitalism – the weak will always suffer and, therefore, in a humane society the state should always intervene in order to support them. However, this is a rather idealistic interpretation of the role of the state. The Welfare State, it has been argued, has been introduced to accommodate the long-term interests of capital, and Offe (1984) suggests that it is introduced as a form of crisis management to reconcile the demands of the people expressed through the democratic political processes with the recurrent crises of a capitalist economy. At the same time this model does reflect the position of exponents of a more egalitarian society, reflected in the work of Rawls (1971) which is discussed later in this chapter.

It will be seen that, at the time when Pinker first proposed this approach there was relative wealth and an optimism that things would get even better in the United Kingdom, so that there was an assumption in the former approach that these residual needy groups would soon disappear, rather than increase in number as they have actually done over the past decade. Even so, the model does have relevance for the education of adults, in as much as it might have been argued that adult literacy was targeted at an apparently small residual group of adult illiterates which would soon disappear. Hence, the Adult Literacy and Basic Skills Unit (ALBSU) was given a renewable grant over the first years of its existence, rather than a permanent one, in order to ascertain the extent to which its services would still be needed after a given period of time had elapsed; although it has subsequently been recognised that this is not a residual problem that will soon go away as schools become 'more efficient' and produce a more literate new generation of adults, but that it is a long-term social problem. The literacy educational process has assumed a different title, adult basic education, and it is now a recognised part of the institutional provision, and ALBSU has assumed a degree of permanence and a continuing grant to guarantee the continuity of its work.

A similar argument could be adduced for ACCESS courses – that is, special courses for the educationally underprivileged to gain access to higher education. It has been argued that they should be state-funded for such time as those underprivileged groups in society fail to achieve in the school system, but when that system finally eradicates the source of need, then the funding can be withdrawn. Whether this will ever be achieved, however, is more problematic and ACCESS courses are becoming more institutionalised, although greater support has been forthcoming for these where there has been local government authorities with a social reformist ideology. Consequently, it may be seen that the institutional welfare approach does reflect a relevant contemporary framework for analysing the provision of the education of adults.

At about the same time, Titmuss (1974: 30–4) produced a threefold model of social welfare, which included these two approaches and also a third:

> Industrial Achievement Model – social welfare institutions are additions to the economy and treat people's needs on the basis of merit, work performance, productivity, and so on.

Certainly some forms of welfare are based upon this approach and it might even be possible to argue that certain forms of education provided by industry and commerce can be analysed from this perspective. For instance, pre-retirement education has been provided by some industrial companies for a number of years, but as the profit margins have fallen during the recent recession such courses have been shortened and even withdrawn. It might perhaps be possible to argue that this industrial achievement model can also begin to account for the fact that grant aid has been withdrawn by the government from traditional liberal adult education. The provision of welfare is an expensive undertaking and the United Kingdom is no longer as wealthy as it was twenty years ago and so there is not sufficient finance to fund every welfare activity (especially when most of the participants of some of them, such as liberal adult education, appear to be able to afford to pay for their own leisure time pursuits!).

Welfare approaches are interventionist and, according to the classical liberal position, they interfere with the basic human rights of the more wealthy, who are taxed more heavily in order to redistribute wealth through welfare, including education. They also argue that helping the underprivileged people in this way prevents them from achieving through their own merit. These arguments will be examined more thoroughly later in this chapter.

Social control models

Since the state must control, it could be argued that any state provision of education is one in which education is being used as a control mechanism. J.S. Mill (1962: 239–40) was very concerned about this when he claimed that:

A general State education is a mere contrivance for moulding people to be exactly like one another: and as the mould in which it casts them is that which pleases the predominant power in government, whether this be a monarch, a priesthood, an aristocracy, or the majority of the existing generation; in proportion as it efficient and successful, it establishes a despotism over the mind, leading by natural tendency to one over the body.

It is perhaps significant to find Carlson (1987: 4) writing in a similar vein about American education:

This first Americanization campaign in the newly independent nation gradually evolved into more formal arrangements for transmitting the national doctrine to the next generation. By the mid-1800s Americanizers in several parts of the nation were well on their way to developing free, tax-supported public schools to further their interests. They wanted schools to bring together children of different backgrounds... for friendly association, for training in the skills that would help them become part of America's middle class society, and for indoctrination in the Protestant republican ideology.

Classical liberalism is here in accord with Marxist analyses of education. Althusser (1972), for instance, regards education as the most significant ideological state apparatus. Freire (1972) also sees formal education as 'banking education', by which he means that students are filled with the predetermined content of a course or lesson, without being given the opportunity to consider alternatives or even to reflect upon the content to which they have been introduced. They are merely expected to learn it and reproduce it. Many other scholars, radicals and non-radicals alike, have recognised that reproduction – both cultural and social – is a function of education. Hence, radical movements have emerged which seek to express viewpoints other than those of the dominant male elites of contemporary society – and these will be more fully discussed later in this book.

There are many examples of the way in which the social control model has been utilised in educational analyses in recent years and amongst the most thorough is Dale's (1989: 65–74) analysis of the Technical and Vocational Education Initiative (TVEI), where the government introduced a scheme through which young adults had resources provided for them for job-related training while they were still at school. The scheme was funded and controlled by the, then, Manpower Services Commission, which was an arm of the Department of Employment. Dale (1989: 113) concludes that:

> Quite crucially, TVEI symbolized and heralded the replacement of a conjunctural with a structural mode of rationality in the politics of education. It centralized control over the allocation of resources and the recognition of demands, and directed them to clear politically, rather than professionally, selected targets.

Overall, the Conservative government in the United Kingdom has endeavoured to exercise control over all forms of education, including universities and adult education, by the way that it has allocated funds. The criterion through which the government has apparently judged education has become economic efficiency rather than effective education. Although it has also introduced mechanisms of quality control, these are as much efficiency driven as they are professionally concerned.

In precisely the same way the emphasis that the government has placed on continuing vocational education rather than liberal adult education in the education of adults may be seen as an extension of this same argument. Indeed, Griffin (1988: 21) draws this conclusion:

> for whereas adult education traditionally reconciled individual needs with those of society, continuing education seems more concerned with reconciling them to society. Thatcher, in rolling

back the state in some of its functions in respect to social welfare, has also rolled back those functions to do with economic policy. Continuing education in Britain, therefore, stands not only for a policy model of education but for a reconceptualization of the whole idea of individual adult learning needs and their incorporation into public policy.

While the Conservative government has rolled back the state in respect to industry and commerce, it has been interventionist in education. Education has become explicitly part of the political agenda of the New Right government (see Jones 1989 for an analysis of this with respect to school education), although it has been illustrated already that education has always been an instrument in government policy. The policies of the United Kingdom government in the 1980s and early 1990s have been designed to re-direct education away from individual needs, to the demands of the industrial and commercial sector of society. If this policy is placed in a global context, however, it might be argued that unless the United Kingdom does orientate itself towards increased industrial productivity, it will continue to become economically poorer in the face of the fierce industrial competition from elsewhere in the world, and then future generations might not be able to enjoy the comparatively high standard of living that the population enjoys at present. Even so, the fact that the rich still get richer (especially those captains of industry who reward themselves with vast pay rises at the same time as they make hundreds of workers redundant) whilst there is an increasing number of poor does raise questions about the nature of a just society, and the extent to which these policies are just.

JUSTICE AND LEGITIMATION

Traditionally, it has been assumed that there is an absolute conception of justice that could be arrived at through rational argument, so that it would be possible to specify the nature of a just society. However, in recent years this approach has been found to be unacceptable and MacIntrye (1988) has argued that there are different traditions and different rationalities, and he suggests that:

> theories of justice and practical rationality confront us as aspects of traditions, allegiance to which requires the living out of some more or less systematically embodied form of human life, each with its own canons of interpretation and explanation in respect

48

of the behaviour of others, each with its own evaluative practices.

(MacIntyre, 1988: 391)

Consequently it can be argued that each of the political traditions that have been discussed in this book has its own approach to the just society and its own rationality for putting it into practice. While it is possible for each to recognise the position of the other, it is difficult for one to change in order to accept another. Indeed, MacIntyre (1988: 396) suggests that such a change would be akin to a religious conversion! At the same time each of these positions may be seen to have certain flaws that make them unacceptable to the other, and this will be briefly illustrated here, rather than arguing for one position as being the one and only form of the just society. In order to do this two major theories of justice, those of Rawls (1971) and Nozick (1974) are commented upon, drawing largely on the analysis presented by Phillips (1986).

Rawls' (1971: 303) general conception of justice is summed up as follows:

All social primary goods – liberty and opportunity, income and wealth, and the bases of self-respect – are to be distributed equally unless an unequal distribution of any or all of these is to the advantages of the least favored.

Rawls (1971: 302) holds that there are two principles of justice:

First: each person is to have an equal right to the most extensive total system of equal basic liberties compatible with a similar liberty for all.

Second: social and economic inequalities are to be arranged so that they are both (a) to the greatest benefit of the least advantaged, consistent with the just savings principle, and (b) attached to positions and offices open to all under conditions of fair equality for all.

Elsewhere (1971: 101) he comments specifically about education:

But the difference principle would allocate resources in education, say, so as to improve the long-term expectation of the least favored. If this end is attained by giving more attention to the better endowed, it is permissible; otherwise not. And in making this decision, the value of education should not be assessed solely in terms of economic efficiency and social welfare. Equally if not more important is the role of education in enabling a person to enjoy the culture of his [*sic*] society and to take part in its affairs, and in this way to provide for each individual a secure sense of his own worth.

Clearly this is a position that exemplifies much of the social reformists' argument, even though it would be possible to argue that the emphasis being placed on continuing and vocational education at the present time is consistent with Rawls' point about education, since it could be suggested that unless the United Kingdom achieves more wealth, it becomes impossible in the long term to provide the facilities for all to enjoy the culture of society and to have opportunity for them to secure a sense of their own worth. At the same time, such provision by the state is contrary to the tenets of classical liberalism! Moreover, any theory of redistribution of resources involves the state acquiring and re-allocating them on other principles than legal individual ownership, so that it violates people's rights. Hence, any provision of education from a welfare standpoint needs to respond to the point that if people's property is legally acquired, by what right should they be unequally taxed in order to be forced to assist others?

This latter position is accepted by Nozick (1974) who is critical of Rawls' work. However, he points out (1974: 183) that it 'is a powerful, deep, subtle, wide-ranging, systematic work in political and moral philosophy which has not seen its like since the writings of John Stuart Mill, if then'. However, another of his reasons for being critical is that it is 'incapable of yielding an entitlement or historical conception of distributive justice'. In other words, Rawls' theory does not provide a rationale for how much or what education the less privileged are entitled to receive – people might have differing viewpoints about this! Indeed, a similar point of view is to be found in Norway, where adult education is very much part of Welfare State provision as a result of the 1977 Adult Education Act (Nordhaug, 1986) and education as a whole is subsidised; however, Nordhaug (1989: 297) also points out that merely providing adult education with subsidies is questionable because:

each participant is in principle subsidised by the government. Better off people get the same indirect economic support as people with small resources. The question then arises whether public transfers should be applied more selectively and concentrated on groups with particularly strong needs rather than being spread over numerous well-off individuals.

Nozick and Phillips do offer other criticisms of Rawls' extremely thorough argument but it is superfluous to embark upon a discussion of those here. Suffice to note that the social reformist position on justice is open to criticisms.

Nozick's own position is of minimal state intervention in order to protect the entitlements of those who have acquired their holdings justly. For him, a just society is one which protects the rights of the population, including their property and wealth rights. However, it is at this point that his argument can be undermined. Phillips (1986: 71–3) raises four significant points, Nozick fails to: provide any justification of individual rights; justify what constitutes a just holding of property; demonstrate that there is still sufficient left for others; show that his theory of freedom is inclusive. Consequently, it can be argued that if the case for the minimal just state is weak, then the case for not providing education for adults on a principle of redistribution of resources is also weak.

If both positions are debatable, as MacIntyre argues, and conceptions of justice can only be understood and accepted from within their tradition, then the policies enacted by the state for the provision of education for adults can always be attacked by those coming from different traditions on the grounds of justice. Indeed, different traditions in society can also express their interest and the state be forced to arbitrate between competing interests – interest group theory will be discussed in a subsequent chapter.

If a just society cannot be agreed upon by all, then those who exercise power through the state will seek to implement their own ideological conception of a just society, or to pursue their own interests, or to enact a combination of the two. Acceptance, or otherwise, of these policies by the population will determine the extent to which the government will command popular support and/or be seen to be legitimate. Held (1984: 301–2) has suggested the extent to which people comply with government policy may be seen on a seven point continuum:

1 coercion – no choice;
2 tradition – do as it has always been done;
3 apathy – cannot be bothered;
4 pragmatic acquiescence – accept fate, even though it is not liked;

5   instrumental acceptance or conditional agreement/consent – go along with things in order to secure another end;
6   normative agreement – what ought to be done in the given situation;
7   ideal normative agreement – what people would like to do.

Held argues that only in the last two cases is there a sense of legitimacy about the situation, although all the others are operative. However, the state need not seem to be too repressive unless the coercion is overt, although the population may well comply with the government for any other of the reasons. At the same time, different groups in the population will respond differently to specific government policies, for as Held (1984: 308) asserts: 'we can say with confidence... that any claim about widespread adherence to a common value system needs to be treated with the utmost scepticism.' Consequently, it may be claimed that no policies about the provision of the education of adults within society will achieve universal support. Its provision, or its lack of provision, depends upon the policies of the governing elite and it will be treated by some of the population apathetically and by others with a sense of pragmatic acquiescence, and so on. Hence, government can use much of the provision of the education for adults to further its policies. But if those policies are not in accord with the interests of other groups, then the provision of adult education becomes a matter of political activity with interest groups looking to government to change its approach. In precisely the same way the state provision of continuing vocational education is being advocated by those who control industry and commerce. In other words, the provision of education for adults becomes an expression of interest in a pluralist society to which the government may respond quite pragmatically in order to appear as either legitimate or responsive to the demands of the people.

CONCLUSION

It has been argued in this chapter that the provision of the education of adults can be understood from the different policy positions adopted by different governments. Additionally, it has been pointed out that there are differing approaches to the idea of a just society, so that any recourse to the idea of justice in discussions about the provision of various types of education demands that the strengths and weakness of each position be thoroughly discussed. Indeed, theories of justice can be understood from within their own tradition as being rational, even though those from other traditions might feel that they are intellectually weak. Finally, it has been suggested that arguments for the provision of any form of education for adults can also be understood in terms of interest group theory, so that organisations like the National Institute of Adult Continuing Education must be viewed as an organisation expressing an interest in society, albeit to a government which does give financial support for its activities.

Society, however, is a complex one, so that the state needs a vast bureaucracy to ensure its smooth functioning and the next chapter focuses upon the bureaucratic state.

REFERENCES

Althusser, L. (1972) 'Ideology and ideological state apparatuses', in B. Cosin (ed.) *Education: Structure and Society* Harmondsworth: Penguin in association with the Open University.

Blamire, J. (1985) 'A Survey of private adult education operators', in *Adult Education* 58(2): 115–21.

Carlson, R.A. (1987) *The Americanization Syndrome: a Quest for Conformity*, London: Croom Helm.

Cohen, Y. (1989) 'The right to educate adults', in R. Tokatli (ed.) *Lifelong Learning in Israel*, Jerusalem: Ministry of Education and Culture, Adult Education Division.

Dale, R. (1989) *The State and Educational Policy*, Milton Keynes: Open University Press.

Fellenz, R.A. (1981) 'The national leadership role belongs to professional adult educators', in B.H. Kreitlow and associates *Examining Controversies in Adult Education*, San Francisco: Jossey Bass.

Field, J. (1990) 'Patterns of autonomy and intervention: the state and workers' education in Britain: 1919–1939', in F. Pöggeler *The State and Adult Education*, Frankfurt: Peter Lang.

Finch, J. (1984) *Education as Social Policy*, London: Longman.

Freire, P. (1972) *Pedagogy of the Oppressed*, Harmondsworth: Penguin.

Griffin, C. (1987) *Adult Education as Social Policy*, London: Croom Helm.

——(1988) 'Continuing education and social policy', in P. Jarvis (ed.) *Britain: Policy and Practice in Continuing Education*, San Francisco: Jossey Bass.

Held, D. (1984) 'Power and legitimacy', in G. McLennan, D. Held and S. Hall (eds) *State and Society in Contemporary Britain*, Cambridge: Polity Press.

Hollins, T. (ed.) (1964) *Aims in Education*, Manchester: Manchester University Press.

Jones, K. (1989) *Turn Right*, London: Hutchinson Radius.

Kreitlow, B.W. and associates (1981) *Examining Controversies in Adult Education*, San Francisco: Jossey Bass.

MacIntyre, A. (1988) *Whose Justice? Whose Rationality?*, London: Duckworth.

Martin, V. (1987) 'Adult education in the shopping centre', in *Adult Education* 59(1): 14–19.

Mill, J.S. (1962) *Utilitarianism – including On Liberty and On Bentham*, London: Fontana.

Moore, A.B. (1981) 'The federal government must assume a leadership role', in B.W. Kreitlow and associates *Examining Controversies in Adult Education*, San Francisco, Jossey Bass.

Nordhaug, O. (1986) 'Adult education in the Welfare State', in *International Journal of Lifelong Education* 5(1).

—— (1989) 'Equality and public policy: ideals, realities and paradoxes', in *International Journal of Lifelong Education* 8(4).

Nozick, R. (1974) *Anarchy, State, and Utopia*, Oxford: Basil Blackwell.

Offe, C. (1984) *Contradictions of the Welfare State*, London: Hutchinson.

Phillips, D.L. (1986) *Toward a Just Social Order*, New Jersey: Princeton University Press.

Pinker, R. (1971) *Social Theory and Social Policy*, London: Heinemann.

Rawls, J. (1971) *A Theory of Justice*, Cambridge, MA: Belknap Press of Harvard University Press.

Russell, L. (1973) *Adult Education: a Plan for Improvement*, London: Her Majesty's Stationery Office.

Thomas, A.M. (1989) 'Legislation and adult education in Canada: a comparative study', in *International Journal of Lifelong Education*, 8(2): 103–26.

Titmuss, R. (1974) *Social Policy:an Introduction*, London: George Allen and Unwin.

4

THE BUREAUCRATIC STATE

When Margaret Thatcher came to power in the United Kingdom one of her rallying cries was to 'roll back the state', and in justification of this policy she frequently cited the size of the bureaucracy needed to run the affairs of the Welfare State and pointed to the fact that this is an expensive operation, the cost of which came from the pockets of the tax-payers. Certainly, the civil service has been viewed by many as a large bureaucratic institution, so that it could justifiably be claimed that the modern state is a bureaucracy. There are certain aspects of bureaucracy that have been transferred to the educational system which is, after all, a part of the state bureaucracy, and in this chapter these will be explained. The first part of the chapter examines the concept of bureaucracy itself, and the remainder of the chapter examines some aspects of bureaucracy that have been introduced into the education system, especially in the education of adults, in recent years, such as literacy, modularisation and standardisation. Finally, there is a brief evaluative comment on these current trends.

THE BUREAUCRATIC STATE

During the period of the Industrial Revolution the division of labour in society, which until that time had been fairly basic, assumed an impetus which has continued to the present day. Whilst the number of different occupations was small and could probably be numbered in hundreds and certainly in tens; now it is to be numbered in hundreds and thousands. Society has undergone tremendous structural changes as a result, such as from a form of mechanical to forms of organic solidarity, as many of the classical sociologists have documented (Durkheim, 1933, *inter alia*).

Industrialisation in the West was accompanied by a number of major social changes, as Kumar (1978) has documented. He highlights urbanisation, demographic changes, decline of community, centralisation, equalisation, 'democratisation', secularisation, rationalisation and bureaucratisation, as being among the other main changes. It will be recalled that one of the characteristics of the state listed in the second chapter was its bureaucratic nature.

Bureaucracy has been the subject of a voluminous literature since Weber first wrote about it. Few writers have surpassed his description of a bureaucratic organisation and so it will be described briefly here. Weber regarded legal authority as being embodied in bureaucratic administration which he (1947: 329–30) suggested has five major characteristics:

1 That any legal norm may be established by agreement or by imposition, on grounds of expediency or rational values or both, with a claim to obedience at least on the part of the corporate group... which in the case of territories is the territorial area....

2 That every body of law consists essentially in a consistent system of abstract rules which have normally been intentionally established....

3 That thus the typical person in authority occupies an 'office'....

4 That the person who obeys authority does so, as it is usually stated, only in his capacity as a 'member' of the corporate group and what he obeys is only the 'law'....

5 [That] the members of the corporate group, in so far as they obey a person in authority, do not owe this obedience to him as an individual, but to an impersonal order....

Elsewhere, in the same volume Weber discusses his conception of three types of leadership: charismatic, traditional and rational–legal, the latter being the bureaucratic leader. Political leaders may aspire to be other than rational–legal, although there have been few charismatic leaders in the political bureaucracy in recent years. (For some in the United Kingdom and elsewhere, Margaret Thatcher might have achieved this status!) Teachers appear rarely to be charismatic since they are required to function within a bureaucratic framework – hence they assume traditional or rational–legal approaches to the performance of their role.

Since Weber wrote there have been numerous studies of bureaucracy and Hall (1963), for instance, studied the work of nine major writers and none listed the same characteristics. Since Hall's work there have been numerous other studies, but there is still no major sense of agreement amongst scholars about what precisely constitutes bureaucracy. It would be tedious and unnecessary to rehearse all of this work here, although it should also be borne in mind that listing traits, without having a theoretical foundation upon which to build the edifice, is an unwise procedure because characteristics can be added or subtracted at will.

However, one approach to bureaucracy that has been used widely in empirical research in recent years has been that developed by the Aston School (Pugh *et al.*, 1972). The six characteristics which they suggest have been drawn from research into a number of organisations and they are employed here. They are:

1 specialisation – division of labour;
2 standardisation – of procedures, roles, and so on;
3 formalisation – of communication procedures;
4 centralisation – of authority;
5 configuration – the shape of the organisation in terms of control;
6 flexibility – the ability to respond to the forces of change (initially, they called this traditionalism).

For the purposes of this study of the bureaucratic state these six characteristics are adopted. It will be seen immediately that a state having these characteristics will have adopted certain policies that will have repercussions for the educational system and three are noted here and discussed in greater detail. Formalisation relates to how those in authority communicate with the population and how the population responds; standardisation relates to the way in which education is provided and certificated; flexibility relates to the manner in which educational courses cannot be adapted for use in the bureaucratic state. Of the other three, there is a specialisation of roles with an increasingly large management structure which relates also to both centralisation and the configuration of the organisation.

FORMALISATION AND ADULT LITERACY

It is commonplace to hear people criticise bureaucracy because 'everything has to be in triplicate'! Indeed, the mode of communication in bureaucracies is formal – that is, it is written communication. Hence, people who are illiterate are unable to take their place in organisations and even play their full role in the bureaucratic state.

Illiterates are denied access to elements of their own culture and to the culture of the wider world. Bethoff summarises Freire's position thus: *'illiteracy* is not merely the inability to read and write, it is also a cultural marker for naming forms of difference within the logic of cultural deprivation theory' (Freire and Macedo, 1987: 3).

Hence, for Freire, literacy has always been a political act but more than that; it has also been one for personal enrichment as newly literate people can play their part in the world:

> Reading the world always precedes reading the word, and reading the word implies continually reading the world. As I suggested earlier, this movement from the word to the world is always present; even the spoken word flows from our reading the world. In a way, however, we can go further and say that reading the word is not preceded by reading the world, but by a certain form of *writing* it or *rewriting* it, that is, of transforming it by means of conscious, practical work. For me, this dynamic movement is central to the literacy process.
>
> (Italics in original)
> (Freire and Macedo, 1987: 35)

Freire's emphasis on transformation, sometimes on political revolution, has meant that not all scholars have supported his activities. The sociologist, Peter Berger (1977: 135–58), for instance, accuses Freire of dragging politics into literacy and claims that Freire's success lies in the fact that he is more orientated to the political than he is to the individual. This demonstrates that it is possible to place a variety of interpretations on different acts, and while Berger is correct to relate politics and literacy his emphasis on dragging politics into literacy suggests that he regards education as a non-political, or an apolitical, phenomenon which is hardly an insightful sociological comment. But if adult literacy were totally revolutionary in nature then no state would be prepared to fund it, however as Levine (1986: 15–16) points out, many literacy programmes in both the developed and the developing world are state funded.

Indeed, the American federal programme helped serve three million people in 1988, according to Beder (1991: 99). He goes on to show (p. 107) that the impact of the federal programme can be assessed under five headings: human capital, basic skill gain, social, attainment of students' personal goals and affect. He points out that there are varying degrees of success with all of these with a considerable advance in basic skills, a positive impact on social participation, that those who completed the programmes tended to achieve their personal goals and that there was a considerable increase in the self-confidence that the students manifest .

However, Beder quite realistically makes the point that unless there was a real increase in human capital gain then the state would not necessarily be prepared to fund the programme. He (1991: 107) writes:

> Rightly or wrongly, demonstrating the impact on human capital is critical to the survival of the federal literacy effort. There are four components to human capital impact: increased employment and increased quality of employment; increased income; reduced need for public assistance; and continued investments by students in further education.

While the studies which Beder reports appear to have a positive effect on all of these aspects of human capital, he makes the point that it is still difficult to prove. For instance, he points out that although many of the newly literate in the New Jersey study on which he reports gained jobs, it was at a time of a rising employment generally, and it is not known whether they would have gained jobs without their adult basic education. None of the evaluations have had control groups, so that the data, while useful, are not conclusive.

Beder (1991: 110) asks whether the impact on human capital is important and concludes that 'it is vital to federal policy' but less so to the students. He notes that: 'Society is willing to subsidize adult literacy education primarily because of its social benefits, benefits which accrue to all through decreased welfare payments and increased economic productivity' (127–8). Now this seems very realistic on the surface and, no doubt, to a great extent his conclusion is justified. However, it is necessary to undertake research with state officials to find out whether the human capital element is the only reason why the state funds adult literacy programmes. Another reason suggests itself when it is recalled that writing is the means of formal communication within, or the language of, a bureaucratic state, and that it is through the written word that the state both communicates with and partly controls the population. It is through writing that inland revenue forms are completed, it is through writing that census forms are returned and it is through writing that instructions are frequently issued, and so on. There is a sense in which illiterates stand beyond the control of the state when its main means of communication are not open to it when it relates to them. It becomes necessary in these cases for the state to employ other means in order to make contact and maintain the means of control over the illiterates, and large numbers of people have to be employed to discover the illiterates and help them to complete their legal obligations. If the bureaucratic state is to control, then it needs a literate population who can be responsive to it. Hence an increase in basic skills through the literacy programme has major significance for the state's activities, and it will be recalled that this was found to occur in Beder's survey.

As the state increasingly adopts computer technology, so it is going to require a 'computer literate' population, and already the idea that computer literacy should form part of adult basic education is being mooted. At the time of writing the state does not yet communicate through computer technology and so it is still an unnecessary addition to the programme. But if computer communication becomes the main method of state communication, then literacy will once again be re-defined and computer literacy will become as significant as the basic skills of reading and writing so that the state will be able to pursue its activities in the formal mode of communication.

FLEXIBILITY, STANDARDISATION AND CERTIFICATION

With the development of technological society, change has become endemic. Indeed, different parts of society are changing at different speeds, with the technological aspects changing 'from hour to hour' (Scheler, 1980: 76). Scheler actually wrote these words in the 1920s, and technological knowledge is changing even more rapidly now than it was then, so that 'half of what most professionals know when they finish their formal training will be outdated in less than five years' (Merriam and Caffarella, 1991: 15). Consequently, a great deal of education and training must necessarily be orientated to this rapidly changing world of technological knowledge and continuing professional education has become central to the educational scene in order to assist people to keep abreast with all the developments in their own field.

The fact that there is an increasing number of continuing vocational courses in the United Kingdom, and elsewhere in the developed world, many of which are certificated is assumed as a basis for the following discussion. That there are so many different courses and awards has led to a variety of new procedures and organisations being established to respond to this situation and to achieve some form of standardisation by the bureaucratic state, three of the most prevalent at the time of writing are discussed here: modularisation, credentialling and credit transfer and national vocational qualifications.

Modularisation and flexibility

In order to respond to the needs of a changing society, the structure of many courses is undergoing change. Amongst the most common themes in education at present is that of modularisation. A module may be defined as a self-contained unit of teaching and learning. It can be used in combination with other modules to build a whole course.

Now a significant thing about a module is that it is flexible; it does not have to be based upon a single academic discipline, but it can be based upon one aspect of life or professional practice and can be either multi-disciplinary or inter-disciplinary. At the same time, it can be single disciplinary, and when it is, the course structure is similar to that of traditional courses whereby students study academic disciplines and sub-disciplines of that discipline, etc. This distinction about the structure of knowledge within a module is really very important and will be discussed further in the next section.

Another significant thing about a module is that it has no fixed length or 'shape'. For instance a module can be a 'long thin' module – which is one which runs through a considerable length of a course, studying a little at a time. By contrast, a module can be a 'short fat' one – that is, one that is studied intensively for a short period of time. In a part-time course, or in continuing professional education, for instance, this could be a single day or two.

Furthermore a course may be designed so that the modules can be strung together, all equal in value and all considered to be of about the same standard, but they can also be like building blocks with foundation courses and then more intensive and higher level courses being built upon the foundations and having a higher value.

Finally, a course may comprise modules taught by different educational institutions, so that a student can study some modules at one educational institution and then move to another, for whatever reason, and continue to study without loss of credit for what had already been studied. In the same way the learners might merely wish to construct their own courses from the modules offered by a variety of educational providers in order to get the type of course that they desire.

The modular structure has considerable advantages for course design and programme planning. It can be used in full-time or part-time courses, in face-to-face education and in distance education and in a combination of different modes of study. It is a standard course and yet a flexible procedure in as much as the same module can be used for a variety of different students, and these can even be taught at the same time – so that it can also become cost effective. Additionally, in continuing professional education, it can be designed very specifically for one or more occupational groups and can be accredited for the amount of time and standard of work achieved, and so on. In this way it allows education to be seen to be relevant to any occupation because the continuing education provision can be 'tailor-made' for the students or clients, and accredited accordingly.

Modular structures are, therefore, standardised, effective, cost-efficient, relevant to specific groups of clients or students and flexible in different delivery systems and even by different providers. Initially, therefore, the modular structure seems ideal for contemporary bureaucratic society. Indeed, it might be claimed that it is the educational structure for a late-capitalist society. It is the product, and has all the hallmarks, of this form of society – but it also has many of its disadvantages!

Accreditation and credit accumulation and transfer

There are two different but related aspects in this sub-section – accreditation and credit transfer. A variety of accreditation agencies are emerging in different parts of the United Kingdom and in this chapter only one is discussed as a case study – the Manchester Open College Federation (Harford and Redhead, 1989). This federation does not provide courses itself but rather it accredits courses submitted to it and awards credits to those learners who complete accredited courses or other accredited episodes of learning successfully. Courses are moderated by paid moderators in order to assess standards, etc. It also accredits other forms of learning design, so that it is much more flexible than the traditional award for a specific course. These credits have different values and classes and as they are collected, so they become a portfolio of accredited learning that the learner has carried out over a number of months or years, and so on. These portfolios can be used in different ways, such as just a record of achievement, as evidence of learning in order to gain admission to higher-level courses and, even, as evidence to be presented to prospective employers. Harford and Redhead (1989: 335) suggest that the Manchester Open College Federation (MOCF):

> exists to improve access to educational opportunities for adults. For such 'students', particularly those whose learning takes place within community settings, the flexible, yet rigorous accreditation system developed by MOCF means recognition by the educational establishments of their achievements. This can act as a spur to further study, as a boost to self-confidence and as an aid to gaining employment for those who want that. It is also a system to the rest of society that recognition of the value of informal education is both desirable and possible.

This approach demonstrates that it is not necessary for the state to be involved in credentialling informal education, although the agencies of state have been much more involved in the credit accumulation and transfer scheme (CATS) that is beginning to emerge nationally between colleges and universities. This idea, known in the United Kingdom as Credit Accumulation and Transfer (CATS), began in North America and was adopted by the Council for National Academic Awards (CNAA) in the United Kingdom in 1986. (The Council for National Academic Awards is being wound up by the current Conservative government and so the future of the CATS scheme has still to be decided, although it is likely that it will be administered by the Open University and that in some way it will almost certainly relate to the national vocational qualifications scheme, which is discussed below). The idea of credit transfer is that credit gained in one course in one institution can be used towards a qualification offered by another institution. Hence, the credit gained by completing one module of a course in one educational institution can be used towards the qualification offered by the same institution at a different time or by another university or polytechnic, and so on. This can only happen if the receiving institution accepts the level of qualification awarded by the first institution for its module. However, if there were to be a national system, then there is no reason why the credit cannot be transferred almost automatically and this is precisely what the CNAA is trying to do. It must be recognised that the CNAA functions at the level of higher education only.

National vocational qualification

The National Council for Vocational Qualifications was established in 1986 to provide a clear framework for vocational qualifications, although the government has presently declared its intention of merging vocational and non-vocational qualifications, so that the aim is now to produce a national credit framework (McNair, 1991). This Council is committed to:

> the creation of 900 National Vocational Qualifications, covering 80 per cent of all occupational areas, by the end of 1992. Initially, it was proposed to introduce the qualifications for the lower four levels, which excluded professional qualifications and vocational qualifications in higher education – which was regarded as level 5. However, the Council is now sufficiently far advanced as to have started on this level as well. When complete the framework is expected to include over 1000 qualifications with over 10,000 separately accreditable units.
>
> (McNair, 1991: 251)

Since this has a vocational foundation its core skills are: communication; problem solving; personal skills; numeracy; information technology; and competency in a foreign language. However, there are problems about the mandatory basis of these skills and so there is still much to be done, but as this system is introduced it will have quite fundamental effects upon the future of the education and training of adults.

In a diverse and complex society, where there is a mass of educational certificates, it has become a bureaucratic procedure to standardise both the accrediting procedures and the awards themselves; hence the emergence of the National Council for Vocational Qualifications and even a move towards the amalgamation of vocational and non-vocational qualifications, so that all fit nicely into a bureaucratic framework. It is then claimed that it becomes possible to adjudge individuals' abilities by their achievement and for those who have certification to feel that they can achieve even greater things, but for those who have no certificates they can be confirmed in their failure and know that it is their own fault that they have not succeeded any further! Or as Dale (1989: 34–5) writes:

> A further characteristic of fundamental importance to educational systems is that bureaucracies recruit on the basis of objective educational qualifications and credentials; the almost universal spread of the bureaucratic form of organization has

placed a major requirement on credentialling on educational systems.

Credentialling is, therefore, one of the ways through which the bureaucratic state and its structures are legitimated and, at the same time, the bureaucratic state and the procedures of bureaucracy underlie much of the movement towards credentialling education; wherever there is bureaucracy there is a need for standardised, written documentation of achievement, even if that achievement is only of something completed rather than any indication of a degree of excellency. The rationality of bureaucratic procedures might thus be seen to have certain disadvantages as well as functional necessities for contemporary society and, consequently, the final section seeks to offer some evaluative comments on these developments.

TOWARDS AN EVALUATIVE ANALYSIS

Thus it may be seen that the procedures of the bureaucratic state find their way into the educational system in a variety of ways and, while this book is primarily about the politics of the education of adults, the final section to this chapter provides an analysis and interpretation of the processes described in this chapter. These will be discussed under six sub-headings: epistemological questions; academic standards; examinations; existential questions; standardisation and legitimation; instrumentalism and rationality.

Epistemological questions

The structure of a module may be single disciplinary or multidisciplinary and it is important that both types of module should be utilised in education. It was certainly suggested earlier that the flexibility of the modular structure is very important to contemporary bureaucracy, but flexibility in itself is not the only quality that should be sought from education. While modular constructions do lead to standardisation, it has to be remembered that not all the knowledge of a sub-discipline, etc. can necessarily be packed into a standardised length module. Indeed, short modules about a single discipline might be misleading for individuals begin to think that because they have mastered one module of an academic discipline, like philosophy, they have actually 'done philosophy'. In this way the significance of the academic disciplines, and even the structure of knowledge, becomes devalued.

Indeed, the relationship between the structures of knowledge and the structures of the presentation of that knowledge requires considerable thought. However, at present, knowledge is being structured and packaged as a marketable commodity, which is itself a symbol of the late modernity.

Academic standards

Although it may not occur, modularisation runs the risk of introducing lower academic standards on at least three counts: that students amass the number of modules rather then pursue a subject at depth; that students follow a variety of subjects rather than a single discipline; that students actually do less work for their awards. It is possible to collect a number of credits and be awarded a degree, for instance, even though all the credits are at a low level. In the same way students can study a variety of unrelated subjects and amass sufficient credits for a degree, even though the comprehensiveness and coherence of the academic programme studied is diminished. In the same way, because a modular course is structured by the number of hours rather than by the demands of the discipline or sub-discipline, the result might be that students actually only study for the prescribed time, rather than become the master of a specified area of knowledge.

Indeed, credit is now awarded for the number of hours studied, rather than the standard attained and this is reducing quality to quantity. Indeed, in the Manchester passport scheme, credit is awarded for attendance as well as achievement and while the opportunity to study and gain additional, or even initial, qualifications is to be welcomed, it is a problematic development to relate credit to time in this manner. Academic standards are hard to define and perhaps impossible to quantify, but they are something to strive for. Bureaucratic procedures are more concerned with completing the process than with the quality of the performance, and it is important that as society moves in this direction academic standards should be retained, even if academics have to resist the moves to quantify standards for the sake of creating smoothly functioning bureaucratic procedures.

Credit is now awarded for competence rather than knowledge, which is also within the nature of bureaucracy. It is to be granted that the traditional emphasis on knowledge went too far in emphasising knowledge to the exclusion of skills, but now the pendulum has swung towards competency based education, and credit is awarded for competence. In itself this is no bad thing, but the concept of competence is poorly defined and varies from one occupation to another, and so there is now standardisation of language but not of phenomenon, and the weaknesses of competency based education are still to be fully worked out. However, it is necessary to discover a way of assessing both knowledge and competence in skills and not to relegate the concept of 'academic' to the insignificant and irrelevant minutiae of everyday life.

These considerations have to be balanced against the fact that credit accumulation and transfer schemes do enable people who are mobile to study and acquire some knowledge and competence, which they might have been denied previously. In addition, more research needs to be undertaken to examine the extent to which, if at all, standards are affected by different approaches and delivery systems.

Examinations and certificates

In Western societies, unlike in Japan, these changes have resulted in a more individuated society, where people have been geographically and socially mobile, and with their specialism they have often sought to change their employment in order to 'better themselves'. This has resulted in a rather anonymous association of individuals – to which Kumar refers as the decline of community – who often have no social identity apart from their occupational one and who need to be able to demonstrate who they are to prospective employers, and others, by their expertise. But rarely do they have opportunity to demonstrate that expertise to a prospective employer, and so the next best things are references and certificates! Sometimes the personal reference, either through face-to-face contract or through the written medium, is useful, but above all prospective employers ask for relevant certification of expertise. However, the mass of qualifications has resulted in an inability to compare qualifications and certificates. Possession of a certificate has now become a passport to future employment – it is interesting that in the Manchester Open College Federation, the portfolio of credits gained by individuals is called a passport. The Portsmouth credit accumulation scheme also uses the same term. The accumulation of credits or certificates is regarded as a passport to other things and places in contemporary individual and anonymous society. Education and training are clearly assuming functions other than those for which they have traditionally been understood. However, the function of the passport is two-fold – it allows some to enter but it debars others. It was Max Weber who first made this point:

> When we hear from all sides for the introduction of regular curricula and special examinations, the reason behind it is, of course, not a suddenly awakened 'thirst for education', but the desire for restricting the supply for those positions and their monopolization by the owners of educational certificates. Today the 'examination' is the universal means of this monopolization and therefore examinations irresistibly advance.
>
> (Gerth and Mills, 1948: 241–2)

Weber's comment does call for educators to examine closely the process in which they are involved since not only are they encouraging access for some, but they may be helping to create a situation which prevents others from participating fully in contemporary society – the process is creating a new educational underclass – every innovation has both advantages and disadvantages, and this is no exception. Certification of education and training courses has functions in society, but it is also a function of the bureaucratic state.

Having been the recipients of information, students are then assessed to discover if they actually have the knowledge. If they can repeat or write it, non-reflectively but correctly, then that is evidence that they have acquired the knowledge. Possession of facts and assessment procedures that test only facts, predominate in many but by no means all educational examinations. Once students have demonstrated that they have remembered what they have been taught they are then given credit for the knowledge that they possess, and carry around their certificates that demonstrate to the public world that they have this knowledge. Modern society now looks for credit, award-bearing educational courses which demonstrate to the world that the learner has acquired specific knowledge or skill or competence. Without the requisite number of certificates students cannot continue to the next level of education – imprisoned in a global classroom (Illich and Verne, 1976) – or enter certain employments. Education now advertises that certain credit is awarded for specific courses and so a market has grown up and education sells its wares (certificated courses). But the fake institutions also undertake a similar exercise and there is a market for bogus certificates and fake qualifications, often purchased at exorbitant prices from pseudo-educational institutions. Even respectable colleges have to award certificates for the shortest of courses so that, through the mechanism of credit transfer, students can construct a portfolio of awards to demonstrate to a sceptical world the amount of knowledge that they have. Even if they no longer possess the knowledge because they might have forgotten it or have rarely used it since its acquisition, it matters not – so long as they possess the certificate; all is well and they have all the evidence that is required. Even if the learning has been forgotten – the certificate must be genuine!

This is no diatribe against certification, although it might appear to be so! This is a criticism of the abuse of what is a necessary system in education. Learning occurs in the private sphere and society and the bureaucratic state are anonymous and, to some extent, de-personalised public phenomena. People move between locations and between occupations. How can applicants for a place on a course or for a job be assessed when they are not known? References can be written about the person, but they may not tell the whole story. How can potential students assess the value of courses that they wish to study, unless there is a reputable certificate at the end? In the public place, certification is a guarantee of something – even if only that the learners attended such a reputable educational institution, or that they once possessed the knowledge or the skills, or that they will be given the opportunity to gain them by following specific courses. Certification, then, is important for all education because of the privatisation of learning and the anonymity of the public world and the bureaucratic state.

Existential issues

It was indicated above that in impersonal bureaucratic society it has become important for prospective employers, and even admissions tutors at universities and colleges, so that they may have something by which to assess a person's previous career. Hence the certificate is very useful in this process. Moreover, it is important for prospective students to know that a course for which they are applying has been accredited by a respectable accrediting agency. It is, therefore, most important for the functioning of modern society to have such a mechanism. At the same time, there is a danger that the certificate becomes more important than the person; that having a certificate becomes more important than the person who possesses it; that the certificate becomes the person; that striving for a certificate becomes more important than the enjoyment of life, and so on. In contemporary society, possession is more important for many individuals than being and, perhaps, education reflects this fact.

Education is a public institution, part of contemporary society and the bureaucratic state and, as an institution it might be argued that it reflects the values of that society. But education is trapped in a dilemma – should it emphasise the having mode of certification or the being mode of the person? It is suggested here, but argued elsewhere (Jarvis, 1992), that it tends to adopt the rhetoric of being but the practices of having, and that this is inevitable because of its institutional status in a bureaucratic state.

Standardisation and legitimation

The diversity of pluralist society is something that no bureaucracy could tolerate. Pugh *et al.* (1972: 32–3) suggest that:

> Standardization of procedures is a basic aspect of organizational structure, and in Weber's terms would distinguish bureaucratic and traditional organizations from charismatic ones.... A procedure is taken to be an event that has regularity of occurrence and is legitimized by the organization. There are rules or definitions that purport to cover all circumstances and that apply invariably.

And so the mass of qualifications and accreditation procedures have to be standardised and there has to be a national accreditation framework, even if that framework hides the complexity of the process. Once in place, however, procedures that are not part of that framework will be deemed to be illegitimate.

Instrumentalism and rationality

Education, then, appears to have assumed the rationality of bureaucracy, but it is worth stopping and asking questions about rationality itself. Indeed, MacIntyre (1988: 9) suggests that: 'rationality itself, whether theoretical or practical, is a concept with a history; indeed, since there are a diversity of traditions of enquiry, with histories, there are.... rationalities rather than rationality'.

If there is no one rationality, then that rationality which is imposed by the functioning of the bureaucratic state is but a position adopted by those who exercise power and, as such, is ideological. Education can be instrumental, geared to ends such as certification and it is rational – but perhaps it is just as rational to have a system of education that seeks to provide opportunities for people to learn and develop, without certification. There are rationalities rather than rationality and so, rationally, there can be a a variety of rationalities underlying different courses in education, and they do not all have to conform to the procedures of the bureaucratic state. This does not mean, however, that through the exercise of government the bureaucratic procedures will continue to dominate and certification and standardisation continue to play a major role in education.

CONCLUSIONS

As an agency of state, education is defined by the state and many of its practices and procedures are controlled and managed by the state. As a social institution, education will also reflect the values of the age and the culture within which it is located. At the same time, within a technological and bureaucratic world, education demonstrates many similarities whatever the country within which it occurs. Education is adapting to the demands of a bureaucratic state and as more states become bureaucratic in their administration, a world of standardised procedures, education follows suit and credentialling and certification of modular courses will probably be discovered in most advanced societies – for the one is but a manifestation of the other.

REFERENCES

Beder, H. (1991) *Adult Literacy: Issues for Policy and Practice*, Malabar: Krieger.

Berger, P.L. (1977) *Pyramids of Sacrifice*, Harmondsworth: Penguin.

Dale, R. (1989) *The State and Educational Policy*, Milton Keynes: Open University Press.

Durkheim, E. (1933) *The Division of Labor in Society*, (trans. George Simpson), New York. The Free Press.

Freire, P. and Macedo, D. (1987) *Literacy: Reading the Word and the World*, London: Routledge and Kegan Paul.

Gerth, H.H. and Mills, C.W. (eds) (1948) *From Max Weber*, London: Routledge and Kegan Paul.

Hall, R.H. (1963) 'The concept of bureaucracy: an empirical assessment', in *The American Journal of Sociology*, 69(1).

Harford, L. and Redhead, S. (1989) 'The credentialling of neighbourhood-based adult education – Manchester Open College Federation in practice', in *Adult Education*, 61(4): 331–5.

Illich, I. and Verne, E. (1976) *Imprisoned in a Global Classroom*, London: Writers and Readers Publishing Co.

Jarvis, P. (1992) *Paradoxes of Learning*, San Francisco: Jossey Bass.

Kumar, K. (1978) *Prophecy and Progress*, Harmondsworth: Pelican.

Levine, K. (1986) *The Social Context of Literacy*, London: Routledge and Kegan Paul.

MacIntyre, A. (1988) *Whose Justice? Which Rationality?*, London: Duckworth.

McNair, S. (1991) 'A National Credit Framework', in *Adults Learning*, 2(9): 251–2.

Merriam, S. and Caffarella, R. (1991) *Learning in Adulthood*, San Francisco: Jossey Bass.

Pugh, D., Hickson, D.J., Hinings, C.R. and Turner, C. (1972) 'Dimensions of organization structure', in R.H. Hall (ed.) *The Formal Organization*, New York: Basic Books.

Scheler, M. (1980) *Problems of a Sociology of Knowledge*, (trans. M.S. Frings), London: Routledge and Kegan Paul.

Weber, M. (1947) *The Theory of Social and Economic Organisation*, (trans. A.M. Henderson and T. Parsons). New York: The Free Press.

5

ADULT LEARNING, EDUCATION AND DEMOCRATIC CITIZENSHIP

No government by a democracy or a numerous aristocracy,
either in its political acts or in its opinions, qualities and tone of
mind which it fosters, ever did or could rise above mediocrity,
except in so far as the Sovereign Many have let themselves be
guided ... by the counsels and influence of a more highly gifted
and instructed One or Few.

(J.S. Mill, 1910: 124)

How critical thinking sustains a healthy democracy.

(S.D. Brookfield, 1987: 51–68)

The quotation from Brookfield is a chapter title which certainly
reflects and represents the approach of many adult educators over the
years and yet there is a clear disagreement between his perspective and
that suggested by Mill. Mill is implying that democracy is not necessarily a good thing, whilst Brookfield's chapter heading suggests that
it is self-evidently good. Clearly Brookfield did not consider the
implications of the type of argument that Mill asserted, neither perhaps should he have done since political argument was not his
purpose. However, there are sufficient implications in this difference
of approach to justify an exploration into the relationship between
the idea of democracy and the functions of adult education and
learning. Indeed, it is a necessary exercise if educators of adults are to
make claims about democracy, or citizenship, and education.

This chapter, therefore, commences with an initial discussion
about the nature of democracy and concludes that no simple definition will suffice. Indeed, the concept varies according to the theories
of and values about society that individual scholars bring to their
analyses. Subsequently, Held's (1987) different types of democracy
are examined. Rather than analysing fully all of his ten types, three

distinct approaches which reflect some of the main tenets of the positions he discusses are examined in order to illustrate something of the complexity of the argument. Finally, it is indicated that the democratic state in some way involves participative citizenship, and so both the concepts of citizenship and citizenship education are discussed.

THE CONCEPT OF DEMOCRACY

The concept of democracy is rather a loose one but in its broadest sense it refers to the fact that in some manner the people have power, or authority, over society. Since it was claimed earlier that the state must control, there must be some relationship between the state and the people, other than one of direct control, if there is to be any form of democratic state. But certain questions need to be asked about the nature of this control, such as – who are the people, do they actually exercise power and, if so, how do they exercise it? Indeed, Lively (1975: 30) raises seven major questions about this rather loose definition of democracy: should all be involved in legislation or only in the decision making process; should the rulers be accountable to the ruled or to their representatives; should the rulers be chosen by the ruled or by their representatives; should the rulers rule in the interests of the ruled? (cited from Held, 1987: 3).

In response to these it can be shown that throughout history the criteria for defining 'the people' have changed – from male citizen to land owner, to educated person, to adulthood over 21 years of age and, finally, to adulthood over 18 years of age. It is not beyond the realms of human imagination to see the possibilities of them being changed yet again. Thus it may be seen how the specific concept of the people has varied over time, but the extent to which the people have ever exercised power is itself debatable; certainly they have sometimes participated in the selection process of the ruling elite and, occasionally, have exercised more direct power in revolutionary-type situations.

These are questions to which further reference will be made below since the above discussion demonstrates that any definition of democracy is itself rather problematic, as Arblaster (1987: 6) claims:

> To suppose that this century can fix the definition of democracy or, even more arrogantly, that it is in this century that democracy has been finally and definitely realised, is to be blind not

74

only to the probabilities of the future but also to the certainties of the past. Hence, any study of what democracy is, any attempt to discover its essence or meaning, must necessarily be an historical study at least in part.

However, throughout history many enlightened and educated persons have suggested that democracy is not necessarily a good form of government. Aristotle certainly had his doubts and so did John Stuart Mill (1910) who claimed that those governments throughout history that had exhibited sustained mental abilities have been aristocratic and, elsewhere that 'no government by a democracy or numerous aristocracy, either in its political acts or in its opinions, qualities, and tone of mind which it fosters, ever did or could rise above mediocrity' (Mill, 1910). Indeed, throughout his writing, he claimed that it was necessary that plural voting should be introduced in order to counterbalance ignorance:

> Until there shall have been devised, and until opinion is willing to accept, some mode of plural voting which may assign to education, as such, the degree of superior influence due to it, and sufficient as a counterpoise to the numerical weight of the least educated class; for so long the benefits of completely universal suffrage cannot be obtained without bringing with them, as it appears to me, a chance of more than equivalent evils.
>
> (Mill, 1910: 287)

Education is one of the ways to enlightenment and whilst everybody should have the right to vote for their leaders, the educated should have more than one vote in order to ensure good government, although he certainly did not regard this as more than a stage in the democratic process. It is, therefore, rather ironic that one of the most influential defenders of education in nineteenth-century England did not regard democracy as necessarily a good form of government and called for more education in order to produce more enlightened citizens, whereas educationalists have tended to regard democracy as a self-evidently good form of government which should be supported.

Clearly this difference of opinion between analysts revolves around a number of the issues mentioned above, including the fact that the definition of the concept has changed, that the social conditions in which the idea of democracy is viewed have also changed and that Mill and educationalists, such as Brookfield and Freire, approach the phenomenon from totally different perspectives. Mill started from the perspective of the upper-class educated liberal elite who did not wish for the unenlightened mass to rule. Freire, for instance, starts from the perspective of the radical Christian who supports the poor in the Third World who do not live in a democratic society and who are defrauded of their humanity by the state and the social system within which they live. Brookfield assumes that people live in a democracy, albeit a representative one, and that critical thought sustains its healthiness. Even more significantly, each of these three thinkers starts from differing ideological beliefs and different theories of society. Both Mill and Brookfield have liberal approaches to society and the individual, and Brookfield's critical thinkers are actually individuals who have the power to think rationally and reasonably rather than being products of emancipation from an apparently false class consciousness. It is the latter who are Freire's concern.

Is it only because of their background and ideology that thinkers differ so much about the concept of democracy, or are there differing value orientations imposed upon the concept itself? Held (1987: 3) suggests that:

> Democracy has been defended on the grounds that it achieves one or more of the following fundamental values or goods: equality; liberty, moral self-development, the common interest, private interests, social utility, the satisfaction of wants, efficient decisions. Within the history of the clash of positions lies the struggle to determine whether democracy will mean some kind of popular power... or an aid to decision-making.... What should be the scope of democracy? To what domains of life should it be applied? Or alternatively, should democracy be clearly de-limited to maintain other important ends?

Since democracy is such a complex phenomenon, it is hardly surprising that people from different historical periods and different social positions have varying understandings of it. Held (1987) identifies nine different models of democracy that have appeared throughout history:

1 Classical democracy – within which citizens enjoy equality so that they can be free to rule;
2 Protective democracy – citizens require protection from government and each other and must ensure that citizens' interests are protected;

3 Developmental democracy (radical) – citizens must be equal and free to ensure collective development;
4 Developmental democracy – political involvement to ensure highest and harmonious expansion of individual capacities;
5 Direct democracy – utopian (see Chapter 9 and below);
6 Competitive elitist democracy – skilled elite chosen by parties;
7 Classic pluralism – government by minorities but political liberty ensured;
8 Legal democracy – majority principle, rule of law to maintain liberty;
9 Participatory democracy – equal right to self-development can only be achieved through participation.

In the last section of his extremely thorough analysis, Held (1987: 290) produces a final tenth model, reflecting some of his own ideas, which he calls a model of Democratic Autonomy, and which he describes in the following terms:

> Individuals should be free and equal in the determination of their own lives; that is, they should enjoy equal rights (and, accordingly, equal obligations) in the specification of the framework which generates and limits the opportunities available to them, so long as they do not deploy this framework to negate the rights of others.

He recognises that as a result of the way that modern society, as well as the state, has developed individuals do not have equal rights in either civil society or the state, so that he (p.283) advocates the need to reform of both. In fact, he calls for a process of double democratisation – civil society needs to be democratised because of the undemocratic power exercised by capital and the state needs to be democratised so that citizens can play their part within its governance. He explains his position by advocating limits and constraints upon both state action and civil society so that the principle of autonomy can be exercised. In this, he points towards a constitution and a bill of rights and responsibilities, and so on. However, there is no need to pursue this analysis further here since it will be returned to in Chapter 8.

It would be possible to expand each of Held's types in order to illustrate ways in which the education of adults relates to each of the different forms of democracy. However, that would produce an over-long analysis. At the same time, it is clear that when claims are made about the relationship between the education of adults and democracy, the complexity of the latter phenomenon has to be recognised. Rather than examining each of Held's types, three approaches to democracy are employed here – one which is individualistic, another which is pluralist and finally a more radical one. Conservatism, in its classical form, does not espouse a democratic approach; Edmund Burke, typified this position when he wrote that a 'perfect democracy is the most shameless thing in the world' (cited from Nisbet, 1986: 44). The three approaches adopted here are similar to Held's developmental democracy, classical pluralism and direct democracy. Each is now discussed in turn.

INDIVIDUALISM, DEMOCRACY AND ADULT EDUCATION

This is Held's developmental democracy which he (1987: 102) explains thus:

> Participation in political life is necessary not only for the protection of individual interests, but also for the creation of an informed, committed and developing citizenry. Political involvement is essential to the 'highest and harmonious' expansion of individual capacities.

In a sense, both Mill and Brookfield fit into this position – a liberal one – and yet they come to it from totally different perspectives .

For Mill society was composed of the sum total of individuals under the jurisdiction of the elected government, and for him individuality was a fundamental element in social well-being. Throughout his essay *On Liberty* he praised individuality as one of the highest forms of the human condition and this is a form of liberalism that is adopted by many well-known theorists of adult education, including Knowles (1980: 24ff.), Rogers (1969: 279ff.) *inter alia*. However, Mill recognised that not all people have the same experiences and achievements (he would have referred to these as different abilities), and reflecting on the way that society was changing he considered that able individuals might get lost in the crowd (Mill, 1910: 123), whose opinion was, he believed, a collective mediocrity. If the uneducated people can vote for their representatives, then representative government will always reflect this lack of sophistication. Therefore, Mill advocated the need for education, so that the representative government could rise above mediocrity. Indeed, Mill went so far as to advocate that while all people, including women (Mill, 1910: 290), which was extremely forward looking for his day, should be given the right to vote; educated people, however, should be able to cast two votes in order to counter-balance the ignorance of the people, or else the mass of people would destroy the individuality of the human condition. Hence, in Mill there is an elitist principle which praised the fruits of education in rather the same manner as Plato's philosopher-kings, and yet there was a democratic principle that called for more education so that the people could be fit to act within a democratic society.

Mill's concept of education was one which reflected the above argument. For him, education was the transmission of those aspects of culture which one generation should purposely choose to transmit to the next, so that people could have their faculties nourished by the richness of the culture of the previous generations. However, this was not to result in the slavish obedience to custom, which he regarded as inhibiting progress, but for the purposes of fostering the proper end of the human condition, quoting Wilhelm von Humbolt with approval:

> 'the end of man, or that which is prescribed by the eternal and immutable dictates of reason, and not suggested by vague and transient desires, is the highest and most harmonious develop-ment of his powers to a complete and consistent whole;' that, therefore, the object 'towards which every human being must ceaselessly direct his efforts, and on which especially those who design to influence their fellow-men must ever keep their eyes, is the individuality of power and development;' that for this there are two requisites, 'freedom and variety of situations;' and that from the union of these arise 'individual vigour and man-ifold diversity,' which combine themselves in 'originality'.
>
> (Mill, 1910: 115–16)

For Mill, then, it might be argued that the traditional liberal adult education should be provided so that citizens might be given the opportunity to develop their powers of reason so that they can play a responsible part in a representative democracy.

In contrast to Mill, Brookfield asserts that it is important to produce critical thinkers through the educational process because the governing elite, who are either the wealthy or those supported by the wealthy, control the state and its apparatuses of information etc. Consequently, the people's interest will only be considered if they are critically aware of the social and political processes that are occurring, and provided that they are active in the expression of their own interest. Hence, Brookfield turns to *The Sociological Imagination* by C. Wright Mills (1970) and suggests that people need to be aware of the social forces that create their private ills. Brookfield maintains that only through critical, sociologically aware thought can people express their own interests and through collective action can they be heard. However, it is to be questioned whether adult education would continue to be provided by the state if it produced critically aware people who sought to oppose the governing elite to any great extent.

However, even if education actually produced critical thinkers, critical thought in itself might not be sufficient to produce action, as the following illustrations demonstrate. The literature of adult education abounds with the feats of people who have devoted their lives to learning. Two instances will suffice for the purposes of this argument – one from the nineteenth and the other from the twentieth century. One of the most adventurous programmes of learning recorded by Kelly (1970), in his excellent *A History of Adult Education in Great Britain*, is that of Thomas Cooper. While not entirely self-educated, Cooper left school at 15 years of age, quite late for the early part of the nineteenth century, and he became a shoemaker. Kelly (1970: 142–3) quotes from Cooper's autobiography:

> I thought it possible that by the time I reached the age of twenty-four I might be able to master the elements of Latin, Greek, Hebrew, and French; might get well through Euclid, and through a course of Algebra; might commit the entire 'Paradise Lost', and seven of the best plays of Shakespeare to memory; and might have read a large and solid course of history, and of religious evidences; and be well acquainted also with the current literature of the day.

Kelly records that Cooper managed this rigorous regime for four years before he had a breakdown which forced him both to give it up and also to leave shoemaking. He then in turn became a school master, a Methodist preacher and a journalist. However, it was during this last occupation that he came into contact with the Chartist movement (c.1838–48), which he joined immediately and in which he became extremely active. Now the Chartist movement was a radical one which sought: the rights of the working classes through suffrage for all men; payment of Members of Parliament and abolition of the law which demanded that Members of Parliament should be property owners; voting by ballot; annual parliaments, etc. This movement, which was seen as radical at the time but by today's standards it was asking for very little more than a representative democratic society, was eventually quashed and people like Cooper imprisoned. There are a number of points to draw out from this illustration that concern the thesis of this chapter, but before this is undertaken, it is necessary to examine another individual learner.

The story of Cornelius Hirschberg is recorded by Gross (1977) and it is from there that this quotation from his autobiography is taken:

> About ten years ago, I decided that I would settle down to a prolonged reading of philosophy. I decided to read Plato and the other ancients in chronological order, and to continue through the years reading at least certain key philosophers, such as Aquinas, Bacon, Spinoza, Leibnitz, Locke, Hume, Kant, Hegel and some moderns. But as soon as I started Plato, I became dissatisfied with my knowledge of Greek history – a discontent which took two years to appease. Such a study of Greek history put me in a state of imbalance with respect to still older history, so reading in Egyptian, Mesopotamian, and Asiatic history became necessary.
>
> I was now forced to consider prehistory. This led to inquiries into the details of the evolution of man, then the animals and plants, and, finally, of the earth itself – a line of reading which would have led me to evaporate into empty space. Fortunately, events made it advisable to refurbish and extend my command of mathematics, which caused several interruptions, adding up to perhaps eighteen months. What became of my philosophy? It is still waiting. Fortunately, those ten years of reading contribute powerfully to the study of philosophy, and if I have a long life, I'll make it yet. I think I can start within two years...
>
> (Gross, 1977: 25)

Hirschberg claims to have read for 20,000 hours, which he says was enough for him to have gained at least five college degrees had he been a registered student. Like Cooper, he was an individual self-directed learner and undertook a course of reading that the vast majority of people would never consider. Whilst Hirschberg originally started on a subject that might well have made him think critically about the ideals of the world, and he says that he learned to read slowly so that he could grasp fully what he was reading, he made no impact upon the social and political structure of his society – but Cooper attempted to, even though not all the subjects that he set himself to learn were ones likely to impinge upon issues of democracy nor was he actually able complete his self-imposed task!

This is one of the major differences between these two remarkable men. But what it also shows is that individual learning need not result in any improvement in the democratic process of society. Indeed, in Hirschberg's case it acted much more like a sedative, for he writes:

> I am stuck in the city, that's all I have. I am stuck in business and routine and tedium. But I give up only as much as I must; for the rest I live my life at its best, with art, music and poetry, literature, science, philosophy and thought. I shall know the keener people of this world, think the keener thoughts, and taste the keener pleasures, as long as I can and as much as I can.
>
> (Gross, 1977: 27)

This is not to decry nor to detract in any way from this tremendous love of learning. It is something to be admired and respected. But, it did not automatically result in either the desire nor the endeavour to create a better and more democratic form of society. His freedom was in the mind. He was free to think his thoughts and nobody, in whatever type of society, could prevent him. He could be critical of what he read, but even if he was a critical thinker it did not need have any effect on the social world or the structures that governed him personally. Of itself, learning is not a sufficient condition for the creation of democracy. What then made the difference with Cooper? Was it motivation, interest, compassion, belief, etc.? Two points emerge that can be pursued further – the first is that Cooper learned of the wretched conditions of the stocking makers in Leicester at that time and it was this that drove him to use his learning within the Chartist Movement. It was not the formal book learning that he had undergone but it was compassion that led to his joining the movement. Second, his own learning might have coincided with his ideological beliefs about social injustice, for he had been a Christian lay preacher and much later in his life he was to become one again. Perhaps the motivating factors for action were his ideology and compassion, not his knowledge. Indeed, there were others in the movement who had not Cooper's learning. This is a point upon which Habermas' (1972) discussion impinges, although he sees this as a fusing of knowledge and interest, and this will be examined further in Chapter 7.

Thus it may be seen that learning *per se* is no guarantee that a healthy democracy will be sustained, even critical thought will not

necessarily do this, since learning might actually act as a social sedative. Even if Brookfield were to be correct, then it must be noted that
he is actually discussing another aim of education to Mill. This is not
an education that is offered to the people so that they can govern, it
is an education offered to them so that they can critically assess
government. Additionally, this is not necessarily a form of education
which any government could easily tolerate. Indeed, Brookfield's
approach contains a very different conception of both education and
democracy to Mill. However, both start with the individual and agree
about the value of education so that the individual can be equipped,
in different ways, to play a part in the democratic processes. Clearly,
there are other ways of looking at this process.

PLURALISM, DEMOCRACY AND ADULT EDUCATION

Pluralism is an approach to society which in its most classical form
emphasises the place of the individual; but in one of its newer forms
it does emphasise the idea of society being made up of a variety of
institutions, each competing with the other and the place of the state
is to respond to these competing interests within society. There has
been a number of variations of pluralism within societies over the past
150 years and so it is unwise even to try to suggest one which would
typify all of them. Held's sixth and seventh models summarise these
different perspectives, that is, competitive elitist democracy and
classical pluralism.

Competitive elitism is a form of neo-pluralism and is perhaps best
illustrated from another of C. Wright Mills' writings, *The Power Elite*
(1959), where he suggests that the leaders of each institution studied
come from the same background, but they still enable democratic
process to occur because they represent competing interests in society. Held suggests that the competing elites model reflects
Schumpeter's understanding of the capitalist market, where the
people elect their leadership whose function is to lead. He goes on to
indicate that such elites are content to have a poorly informed or an
emotional electorate. In other words, this form of pluralism is not one
which will happily support an assertive electorate or liberal adult
education of the type espoused by Brookfield. However, it is one
which seeks professional expertise and it relies on the advice of the
expert.

By contrast, Held (1987: 204) justifies classical pluralist democracy
in the following manner:

[It] secures government by minorities and, hence, political liberty.
[It is a] crucial obstacle to the development of excessively powerful factions and an unresponsive state.

Unlike the previous type, this form of pluralism anticipates that there are some citizens who play an active role in the affairs of state, so that those who exercise power might be supportive, to some degree, of an educational process which would enable citizens to perform that role in a more informed manner. In addition, it could be argued that whenever interest or pressure groups have existed within society, and their very existence is a symbol of a pluralistic form of democracy, then they might also espouse non-formal educational approaches in order to get their message to their potential adherents. Their technique is often of a *banking* approach to education, or education from above, by educational theorists whether they are radical, like Freire, or reformist, like Brookfield, so that the educational method in itself need necessarily have no relationship to the wider world – a point well made by Giroux (1981) – although it must be acknowledged that dominant ideologies sometimes utilise educational methods that reflect their own ideological position.

Significantly, however, in late modern society the individual appears to play a greatly reduced role, so that citizenship becomes an apparently less important concept and democracy appears to be at least one stage further removed from the people.

RADICALISM, ADULT EDUCATION AND DEMOCRACY

Held regards this as the end of politics position, which will be discussed more fully in a later chapter of this book. He writes of it (1987: 136):

The 'free development of all' can only be achieved with the 'free development of each'. Freedom requires the end of exploitation and ultimately complete political and economic equality; only equality can secure the conditions for the realization of the potentiality of all human beings so that 'each can give' according to his or her ability and 'receive what they need'.

This is the utopian Marxist position, so that the final illustration of this discussion must be taken from the work of Paulo Freire. However, there was no pluralism in Freire's analysis of society – he treats the political elite rulers as a single elite whilst the remainder of the people are ruled over. There is no chance of the people exercising power. The mass of people are hardly represented, rather they are exploited and oppressed by the propertied class (Freire, 1972). Even where education is offered to the masses, it is a form of 'banking education' in which the people are manipulated to accept the interpretation of reality with which they are presented. As Freire (1972: 48) writes:

> The banking approach to adult education, for example, will never propose to students that they consider reality critically. It will deal instead with such vital questions as whether Roger gave green grass to the goat, and insist on the importance of learning that, on the contrary, Roger gave green grass to the rabbit. The 'humanism' of the banking approach masks the effort to turn men into automatons – the very negation of their ontological vocation to be more fully human.

This is the classic Marxist-type analysis of society in which there is only one way for the people to gain power, by revolution. This entails a new approach to education, one with which not all adult educators are happy since they do not wish to see education labelled as a revolutionary tool, and yet it is one which is similar to that advocated by Brookfield. Freire advocates that students and teachers should enter a dialogue – the education of equals (Jarvis, 1985) – in order to begin to teach and learn from each other in a critically aware manner. More liberal thinkers are able to concur with Freire when he discusses critical awareness, and so on, but Brookfield appears to be more concerned about the individual than about society, and he also ignores the content of the critical process. Freire starts with the oppressed people's actual concerns, those which he has learned about in the dialogue. These concerns are much more overtly political. He also uses a problem-posing method, making reality a problem to be understood and he recognises that this has a revolutionary perspective. However, it must be pointed out at this time that Freire does not prove that the teaching technique is the cause of the changes that he was able to produce, and it could be argued that the style and the ethos are as significant as the method. But it is much more than just method, or style and ethos, for the learning to be complete there must be praxis – a fusion of thought and action. Following the radical learning, there must be radical action, in order to produce a better world in which all people might live.

For Freire, education has to be empowering and liberating. Freire does not write about democracy because the society in which he worked was clearly not one. He does not envisage a representative democracy at the end of the process but a utopian society in which people are free to become more human and to humanise their world. Then the people have power and, in a sense, this is what democracy is in its essence – but it is a more radical interpretation. Nevertheless, Freire's concerns about humanising the world are the concerns of citizenship, and the final sections of this chapter look briefly at the idea of citizenship education and citizenship itself.

CITIZENSHIP EDUCATION

To conclude this discussion, it might be asked whether adult education has ever contributed directly to the development of any form of democracy, and this becomes a difficult question to answer since there are few well-known examples where it might have occurred. Among the finest examples are, perhaps, the foundation of the folk high school movement and the Canadian adult education involvement in Canada's reconstruction process during and after the Second World War: in the former adult education was an instrument of the state whereas, in the latter, adult educators took the lead from the politicians and it is not surprising, therefore, that Selman (1991) focused upon the relationship between citizenship education and the adult education movement in Canada.

In the nineteenth century, when there was an encroachment of German culture into Danish territory, a different form of pluralism existed for a while, a pluralism of cultures and of states, and one of the Danish responses to the dominance of the German culture was to found a new educational movement – the folk high school movement. This educational movement was committed to a single major task, that of the preservation of the Danish culture, in order to preserve the young liberal democracy which was emerging in Denmark. Hence there was an allegiance of state and civic society for the preservation of the latter, and this allegiance is something that has continued to the present day in certain aspects. (See Thomas, 1982: 24–32 for a fuller discussion of this.)

One significant thing about the form of education which was espoused by the folk high school movement was that it employed the lecture method, getting the students to learn about the richness of the Danish culture and to appreciate that cultural wealth. This was a similar form of education to that advocated by Mill, but this time its aim was not to prepare an elite to elect a government, but to prevent a stronger culture from overcoming a weaker one, to preserve the weaker culture within a cultural pluralism.

An illustration from Canada's history is also used here to illustrate another involvement of adult education in citizenship and it comes from the period of the Second World War. During the catastrophe of this period Canada, like many countries, was in a turmoil, although naturally not actually enduring the problems of the violence that Europe and Asia were experiencing. However, there seemed to be a feeling that after the war Canada's reconstruction could be manipulated in dangerous ways and Canadian adult educators were concerned about the loss of democracy that might result, unless there was an informed populace. It, therefore, established a Special Committee on Education for Reconstruction with a mandate to prepare for the Canadian Association of Adult Education a policy as to how this might be averted. The upshot of the committee was that it believed:

> that unless Canadian public opinion and public will was mobilized through every available agency and medium Canada would drift into the postwar world without any clear social purpose. The Committee thought that this critical situation demanded courage to pool what vision ... they might have, and face realistically the facts of the existing situation.
>
> (Welton, 1987: 25)

Believing that there was a narrow controlling interest underlying Canadian society, the Committee recommended a conference to be held in September, 1943. The task of that conference was to plan a campaign of public education which they did. Citizens' Forum was founded, groups engaged in a dialogue with the world became active throughout many parts of Canada, and the founders believed that only through having an informed citizenry would citizens be freed and would Canada emerge from this period with any semblance of democracy. Whilst Welton (1987: 29) claims that their 'vision awaits fulfilment' the adult education movement in Canada acted as an organisation in order to begin a democratic process. However, it must be pointed out that in this instance it was the movement acting in a political manner as well as an educational one, as a political interest group at the time when the governing elite was otherwise engaged with the war itself, that became the instrument of democracy and not adult education alone.

There is a number of movements which either use educational means or are educational movements which engage in political action that may be regarded as forces for democratisation of society: of the former type is the National Issues Forum sponsored by the Kettering Foundation in the United States which provides educational material on specific issues, chosen annually, in order to produce an informed citizenship on these topics, which are then debated with the politicians in Washington each year; and of the latter type the Highlander Centre founded by Myles Horton in Tennessee is perhaps the best known. Perhaps less well known is that Highlander actually runs citizenship schools (Peters and Bell, 1987). Indeed, a number of similar activities are recorded by Tjerandsen (1980) and, more recently by Boggs (1991). This latter book is, however, more concerned about adult civic education, claiming to be the only book of its kind. Both of these books, however, recognise the complexity of the issues that are involved in citizenship education today, especially as there is such a diversity of beliefs and practices, but they tend to assume that citizenship can only be exercised in this participative and active manner. This is clearly not the only way that citizenship has been viewed, given the diversity of forms of democracy that have been discussed in this chapter and the diversity of political traditions mentioned elsewhere in this book. Hence, it is necessary to explore briefly the concept of citizenship here.

'Citizenship', writes Barbalet (1988: 1), 'is as old as settled human community. It defines those who are, and who are not, members of a common society'. But, as he goes on to point out, in the state:

> The issue of who can practise citizenship and on what terms is not only a matter of the legal scope of citizenship and the formal nature of the rights entailed in it. It is also a matter of the non-political capacities of citizens which derive from the social resources they command and to which they have access. A political system of equal citizenship is in reality less than equal if it is part of a society divided by unequal conditions.

Hence the nature of the questions now being asked are about participation in the common society and its governance, but also about whether this is undertaken as a right of citizenship or not. Clearly this relates back to the nature of the state and a number of theorists have endeavoured to demonstrate the way different concepts of citizenship have related to different political traditions. Turner (1990) has ident-ified two variables in this process: the passive–active dimension, that is, whether citizenship is developed from above in relation to the state or below in conjunction with participatory institutions such as trades unions; the relationship between the public and private arenas in civil society. He suggests that a conservative view of citizenship is as passive and private, while a more revolutionary form is active and public. By combining these two dimensions he gets four forms of citizenship:

Citizenship

Below	Above	
Revolutionary contexts	Passive democracy	Pubic space
Liberal pluralism	Plebiscitary authoritarianism	Private space

Source: Turner, 1990: 200.

Boggs' (1991) discussion on adult civic education assumes a liberal pluralist conception of citizenship. Freire's (1972) discussion clearly approaches the revolutionary context. The Antigonish movement might be another that can be seen in this context (Crane, 1987). The New Right political parties which have governed the state in the 1980s have almost demanded as passive form of citizenship, where citizens have done their duty when they have given a mandate to the governing elite to manage society for a specified period of time. In 'plebiscitary democracy, the individual citizen is submerged in the sacredness of the state which permits minimal participation in terms of the election of leaders, while family life is given priority in the arena of personal ethic development' (Maier 1988, cited by Turner, 1990: 209).

Any form of citizenship education of adults, if developed from above in relation to the state, will clearly have totally different perspectives and refer to such ideas as obedience to the established authority and practical issues, and so on; whereas that developed from below in relation to participation might well concentrate upon rights and interests and so on. The former will tend to contain less democratic perspectives on the state and fall into the conservative or liberal traditions (of the New Right variety), while the latter will be more democratic and cover the spectrum of political tradition from the more traditional liberal through social reformism to radicalism.

Hampton (1990: 10) has suggested that in the United Kingdom the past 20 years have witnessed a swing from a participative to a passive approach to citizenship:

> The approach of the 1980s was to reduce the reliance on state provision and to emphasise the role of the individual as consumer rather than citizen. In this context, educational support for people who become more active in relation to services previously understood as 'public' may change its character.
>
> In the 1970s, the emphasis was placed on discussion of how to enable people to participate more widely in the provision of public services. In both periods the intention was to expand the concept of citizenship – more people were to be involved in a wider range of public activities. Although inherently controversial, the role of adult education was clearly to enable people to contribute more effectively to the political process as active citizen.

As Hampton points out the New Right wanted citizens who were active as consumers of what the state and private concerns provided, so that issues such as 'checking school accounts' (Hampton, 1990: 11) become important as citizenship issues but not those issues of educational policy. Adopting the latter participative perspective, even if it be peaceful and liberal, might well conflict with those who control the apparatuses of state, especially if they hold the opposing views of 'good' citizenship! At this point, it might be seen how easy it becomes to undermine the social stability of society – the more authoritarian and bureaucratic the state, and those who control it, the less able it is to cope with participative forms of citizenship but the more reformist the state the more it will encourage such approaches. This is also reflected in those types of education of adults which receive formal support from governments; when government seeks one form of citizenship it will sponsor one form of education and when the government changes a new form might find favour. The content of education, then, changes with the policy of government, but formal or funded education of adults is usually part of the way in which government policy is enacted. The education of adults is, therefore, inextricably bound up with government policy.

CONCLUSIONS

This chapter started by contrasting the power of the state with the power of the people in democracy. It highlighted the potential paradox about the nature of the state that was discussed earlier in this book – by its very nature the state must control so that it divides the people into the rulers and the ruled which raises fundamental questions about the nature of democracy. There is essentially a division at this point, and this is demonstrated most clearly in terms of citizenship and citizenship education. But it also highlights the very essence of the political processes – that there is always a potential conflict between those who are in authority and those who are managed, between the rulers and the ruled. Those who rule claim the right to distribute all forms of scarce resources to the ruled, but the ruled might feel that the distribution process is unjust and, consequently, they endeavour to gain more usually by peaceful means although in the same way as the use of force should be the last resort of the rulers, force and revolution are always the last resorts of the ruled.

Within Western society a form of participation has been arrived at, representative democracy, but in recent years the individual appears to have decreasing influence, so that liberal adult education may have become less political and more of a leisure time commodity for those who are interested in purchasing it. At the same time, questions about human rights and individual and group interests, are again beginning to be asked. However, these rights are not necessarily granted, nor are people always free to pursue their own interests, so that the nature of society is one of tension and struggle and potential conflict, rather than peace, harmony and goodwill. The education of adults has also been involved in this struggle and this is discussed in the following two chapters.

REFERENCES

Arblaster, A. (1987) *Democracy*, Milton Keynes, Open University Press.

Barbalet, J.M. (1988) *Citizenship*, Milton Keynes: Open University Press.

Boggs, D.L. (1991) *Adult Civic Education*, Springfield, Illinois: Charles C Thomas.

Brookfield, S.D. (1987) *Developing Critical Thinkers*, San Francisco, Jossey Bass.

Crane, J. (1987) 'Moses Coady and Antigonish', in P. Jarvis (ed.) *Twentieth Century Thinkers in Adult Education*, London: Croom Helm.

Freire, P. (1972) *Pedagogy of the Oppressed*, Harmondsworth, Penguin.

Giroux, H.A. (1981) *Ideology, Culture and the Process of Schooling*, London: The Falmer Press.

Gross, R. (1979) *The Lifelong Learner*, New York: Touchstone Books.

Habermas, J. (1972) *Knowledge and Human Interests*, London: Heinemann.

Hampton, W. (1990) 'Adult education and the active citizen', in *International Journal of University Adult Education*, XXIX (1): 3–14.

Held, D. (1987) *Models of Democracy*, Cambridge: Polity Press.

Jarvis, P. (1985) *The Sociology of Adult and Continuing Education*, London: Croom Helm.

—— (ed.) (1987) *Twentieth Century Thinkers in Adult Education*, London: Croom Helm.

Kelly, T. (1970) *A History of Adult Education in Great Britain*, Liverpool: Liverpool University Press.

Knowles, M.S. (1980) *The Modern Practice of Adult Education*, Chicago: Association Press.

Lively, J. (1975) *Democracy*, Oxford: Basil Blackwell.

Maier, C.S. (ed.) (1988) *Changing Boundaries of the Political*, Cambridge: Cambridge University Press.

Mill, J.S. (1910) *Utilitarianism, Liberty and Representative Government*, London: J.M Dent.

Mills, C. Wright (1959) *The Power Elite*, New York: Galaxy Books.

Nisbet, R. (1986) *Conservatism*, Milton Keynes: Open University Press.

Peters, J.M. and Bell, B. (1987) 'Horton of Highlander', in P. Jarvis (ed.) *Twentieth Century Thinkers in Adult Education*, London: Croom Helm.

Rogers, C.R. (1969) *Freedom to Learn*, Columbus, OH: C.E. Merrill.

Selman, G. (1991) *Citizenship and the Adult Education Movement in Canada*, Vancouver: Centre for Continuing Education, University of British Columbia in co-operation with the International Council for Adult Education.

Thomas, J.E. (1982) *Radical Adult Education: Theory and Practice*, Nottingham: Dept of Adult Education, University of Nottingham.

Tjerandsen, C. (1980) *Education for Citizenship*, Santa Cruz: Emil Schwarzhaupt Foundation.

Turner, B.S. (1990) 'Outline of a theory of citizenship', in *Sociology* 24(2): 189–218.

Welton, M. (1987) 'On the eve of a great mass movement', in T. Cassidy and R. Faris (eds) *Choosing Our Future*, Toronto: OISE Press.

—— (1970) *The Sociological Imagination*, Harmondsworth: Pelican.

6

THE PEOPLE'S RIGHTS

Article 26
(1) Everyone has the right to education. Education shall be free, at least in the elementary and fundamental stages. Elementary education shall be compulsory. Technical and professional education shall be made generally available and higher education shall be equally accessible to all on the basis of merit.

(2) Education shall be directed to the full development of the human personality and to the strengthening of respect for human rights and fundamental freedoms. It shall promote understanding, tolerance and friendship among all nations, racial and religious groups and shall further the activities of the United Nations for the maintenance of peace.
(The Universal Declaration of Human Rights,
December, 1948)

In the United Nations' *Universal Declaration of Human Rights*, education is specified as a right, but it will be recognised from the earlier chapters that since the state must control, the concept of rights becomes problematic. Are there rights, for instance, that are over and above the power of the state? Are there different forms of rights? Questions like this demand discussion. Consequently, the first part of this chapter explores the concept of rights, and it is later argued that adult education might be viewed as a right of citizenship. However, citizenship rights are not automatic, but part of the struggle between rulers and ruled that constitutes the normal social process. It will be argued here that these rights are disbursed by the state at specific times in history, especially when the elite need the support of the people, and three case studies will be employed to illustrate this point. At other times, however, the state seeks to claw them back. The chapter concludes with a brief discussion on the Bill of Rights for the Adult Learner which was developed by the Board of Directors of Adult Education Organizations in the United States in 1991.

THE CONCEPT OF RIGHTS

A director of a Japanese company training school was recently asked by the author, whether the members of the company for which he worked had the right to attend his centre for training, and the director's response was: 'they have no rights to attend, only a duty'. This typifies a problem surrounding the concept itself and which is also inherent throughout this study: is it only the company that has the right to demand that its employees receive training, but not the right of the employees to ask for it? Who decides what is a right? In a similar manner, is it only the state that has the right to demand that its citizens accept what it decrees or do its citizens have rights within the society? Indeed, what is a right, and even are there any rights at all?

White (1984: 17) describes the variety of approaches to the idea of rights:

> A right as such is something one can have or be given, earn, enjoy, or exercise. It is something one can claim, demand, assert, insist on, fight for, or secure or what one can waive, surrender, relinquish, or forfeit. It can be recognized and protected or disregarded, altered, abridged, infringed, whittled away, violated, or trampled upon....

It might well be asked, therefore, whether there are actually any rights at all? To this, Gewirth (1984: 91) might respond that it is widely held that there are no absolute rights, and even the right to life may not be absolute, although he thinks that there are absolute rights within carefully defined limits. For instance, it may under very exceptional conditions be right to take a life to prevent that person from killing innocent people. However, even this point is disputable. Gewirth, however, goes on to try to dispute this by finding situations where the right is absolute and he concludes that, in his opinion, there are situations where absolute rights obtain. However, all of these situations involve both the right to life and not to be killed through torture by close relatives. (See also Nozick's (1974) similar argument to this.) Indeed, these are fundamental issues of a moral nature and might command near universal assent, but it is more likely that if such events occur they would command even more universal condemnation.

However, it is still difficult to prove beyond any doubt that any right is absolute, because it is moral. Indeed, Frankena (1963: 23) suggested that no rule can be framed that does not admit to exceptions. Nevertheless, morality is one of the firmest grounds upon which it is possible to argue for absolute human rights. However, it is perhaps more possible to argue that absolute laws are problematic even though there might be an absolute good; but to argue for an absolute good, such as caring love, goes beyond the scope of this chapter and, in any case, even if caring love is an absolute good there may still be no logical reason why people should care or put it into practice.

Even if it is possible to claim that people, as a result of either conception or birth, have the absolute right to live, if there is no food and water then those rights become meaningless. Even if absolute rights could be proven beyond reasonable doubt, it does not mean that they will necessarily be honoured or respected. Starving people in Ethiopia may have the right to live and there may be sufficient food in the world to feed all the starving people in that country, but if there is not the political will to give the aid then the people starving will die.

The extent to which rights will be fulfilled depends upon the social situation. MacDonald (1984) also noted that it is difficult to enjoy human rights in the solitude of a desert island, so that they are inherently social in character, and if they are social then they are political! But it may not be the right to life, or the right to food but the right to speak freely or the right to assemble with others for which the people struggle. These rights may in no way be absolute; they are of a different type and are more political/legal than the former ones. White (1984: 16) pointed out that:

> Rights can be distinguished as moral or legal, religious or political, statutory, constitutional, customary or conventional, epistemological or logical, etc. Thus one may have a moral, but not a legal right to oppose a certain measure; a statutory right to a state pension.....

However, when the concept of right is extended from the absolute to the everyday, then it is necessary to ask again what constitutes a right. Waldron (1984: 15) suggested that there are three ways that rights might be understood: a particularly important interest; interests given lexical priority over other interests; rights which are the basis of strict constraining forces on action. This final form is typified by Gewirth's argument above, and by the fact that the minimal statists, like Nozick, would argue that it is only in extreme circumstances that the state should exercise its power to ensure that people's absolute rights are protected. Whereas Rawls would argue for the second type, that the state should intervene more frequently to protect those special interests to which priority has been given in order to reach a commonly agreed conception of justice in society. Hence some countries, such as the USA, have incorporated certain rights into laws.

Waldron's first category is of particularly important interest, but the question that must then be asked is to whom is this interest particularly important? If it is important to relatively few people, for instance, it is most unlikely to be recognised as a right by the state or the population as a whole. Nevertheless, this does not stop those who hold to the minority interest trying to persuade others of the importance of their position, and this will be discussed more fully in the next chapter.

Rights, then, are clearly about political morality and about the struggle that exists between the ruled and the rulers in the allocation of certain freedoms or resources, and for the purposes of this chapter emphasis will be placed on the political, on those rights that are granted to citizens. (While these may also be moral, there is no intention here to enter the ethical debate about adult education.) Citizens' rights may cover all three of Waldron's categories but especially those which might be regarded as priority interests. Turner (1990: 190) summarises this position, relating citizenship rights to democracy:

> While the notion of abstract Human Rights (possibly in association with some commitment to Natural Law) no longer commands widespread intellectual support, it is clear that the institution of definite 'rights' is an essential feature in the protection of public space as an arena of legitimate debate. The secular institution of right cannot, therefore, be separated from the question of democracy; and the infrastructure of democracy is a fundamental, if limited, restraint on the employment of coercive force. It is 'the democratic apparatus, which prevents the agencies of power, law and knowledge from fusing into a single leading organ' (Lefort, 1988: 29).
>
> (Turner, 1990: 190)

However, rights of citizenship are not self-evident nor are they necessarily natural. To some extent, therefore, it depends on a variety of factors as to what people will regard as rights, such as their place in the social structure, their ideology, and so on. Consequently, there will most likely be some tension between the rulers and the ruled in respect of what the ruled are given as their citizenship right. Moreover, there are likely to be tensions within civil society between those who control capital and those who do not so that, following Marshall (1981), there are inevitable tensions between the demands of state, capital and welfare – or, the political, the civil and the social. But these tensions will vary depending on a variety of factors including the political ideology of those who control the state, so that those having a conservative or traditional liberal understanding are not likely to place a great deal of emphasis on the social, as reformists and radicals are. But in any form of democracy the rulers do demand some support from the ruled, so that even when minimal statists are in power they are likely to provide certain social rewards at times when that support is most needed – like the Chancellor of the Exchequer giving away financial inducements in the Budget before a General Election, even though they are not called that and its practice is frequently denied! To paraphrase Dworkin (1984) the promise of rights seems to be a 'trump card' which the elite play to win the people's support.

It is suggested here that education, especially in its traditional adult liberal form, may be regarded as one of these social rights of citizenship but because of its very nature, it is likely to be seen as something of a 'political football'! In order to examine this theory it is useful to look at four case studies of when adult education has been regarded in this light. Having done this the chapter proceeds by examining the social processes by which society functions and rights are granted and then looks at the result of the promise of educational rights and examines the situation after the promise is made. The chapter then concludes with a brief discussion of the 'Bill of Rights for the Adult Learner'.

FOUR CASE STUDIES

Case study 1

Immediately following the French Revolution, Condorcet (1792) presented the following proposal for educational reform and national instruction in which the state should:

> Offer to all human individuals the means to fulfil their needs, assure their well-being, know and exercise their rights and to understand and fulfil their duties. To assure to every one of them the opportunity to perfect their job, to enable them to execute

the social functions to which they are called, to develop the whole range of the talents that they have received from nature and, by all of this, to establish a real equality among our citizens ... this has to be the first goal of national instruction.... We have, finally, observed that instruction should not abandon individuals at the moment they leave school; that it should embrace all ages; that there should be no age where learning is impossible or useless, and that this second instruction is all the more important in view of the fact that childhood education has been enclosed within narrow bonds. Furthermore, instruction has to be universal, i.e. reach out to all citizens. It has to be diffused with equality permitted by the budget ... it has to encompass all human knowledge, and assure the people, at any age, the ability to retain their knowledge or to acquire new knowledge.

(Cited in a slightly modified form in Leirman, 1990: 19)

Case study 2

Having examined that statement by Condorcet, consider this long quotation from the introductory letter of A.L. Smith to the Prime Minister in the famous 1919 Report of the Adult Education Committee of the Ministry of Reconstruction in England:

(ix) The Committee has based its conclusions upon the following propositions:

1. That the main purpose of education is to fit a man [*sic*] for life, and therefore in a civilised community to fit him for his place as a member of that community.
2. [...] all education must be for citizenship – that is the rights and duties of each individual as a member of the community; and the whole process must be the development of the individual in his relation to that community.
3. That the essence of democracy being not passive but active participation by all in citizenship, education in a democratic country must aim at fitting each individual progressively not only for his personal, domestic and vocational duties, but, above all, for those duties of citizenship....
4. [....]
5. That the necessary conclusion is that adult education must not be regarded as a luxury for a few exceptional persons here and there, nor as a thing which concerns not only a

short span of early manhood, but that adult education is a permanent national necessity, an inseparable aspect of citizenship, and therefore should be both universal and lifelong.

6. That the opportunity for adult education should be spread uniformly and systematically over the whole community, as a primary obligation on that community in its own interests and as a chief part of its duty to its individual members....

Case study 3

Examine now the following statement in the 1944 Education Act in the United Kingdom:

Section 4.1: Subject as hereinafter provided, it shall be the duty of every local education authority to secure the provision for their area of adequate facilities for further education, that is to say:

a. full-time and part-time education for persons over compulsory school age; and
b. leisure time occupation, in such organised cultural training and recreative activities as are suited to their requirements, for any persons over compulsory school age who are able and willing to profit by the facilities provided for that purpose.

Case study 4

Consider also China, after the Japanese invasion and the establishment of the communist system in 1949: the first National Conference on Worker–Peasant Education was convened in 1950. The Conference pointed out that:

The central task at present for the nation is to restore and develop rapidly the country's production and construction, which depends mainly on two forces of workers and peasants on the production front. If educational work does not co-operate to heighten the ideological consciousness and raise the level of culture and techniques of the two main forces, the new attitude toward labour and the creative spirit required by the production and construction will not arise, which will do harm to the central task; and our educational work will lose contact with reality.

(Yao Zhongda, 1987: 16)

As a result throughout China there was a tremendous growth in all forms of adult education provision, not only for work but also for literacy and other forms of education. Yao Zhongda claims that this lasted a long time and yielded remarkable results, but it ceased with the Cultural Revolution.

In each of the four cases mentioned, there are common factors – after the crisis, be it war or revolution, there was – among other things – an appeal to build a new nation and many proposals were put forward about the way in which this might occur, including a promise of more education, and the education of adults is specifically mentioned. In the first case, there was talk of education as a right, in the second it referred to citizenship, in the third there is just the statement in law that the state has a duty to its citizens and in the final one case, there was a tremendous attempt by the state to enrich the lives of the people through education, until the cultural revolution put a stop to it. The first and last cases follow a revolution while the middle two follow a war, and this is important to the following analysis.

Even consider the date of that famous *Universal Declaration of Human Rights* with which this chapter began; it was 1948 and just after the Second World War, and so once the crisis was over there was to be at least a new earth, even if the new heaven was not so easily obtained! However, universal human rights are harder to enforce, because there is no universal system to ensure that they will be enacted. Whilst they may be recognised by the governments which sign the declarations, the governments still exercise sovereign power within their own states and there is no way of compelling them to enact a law to put into practice what they have signed in a declaration. The relationship between human rights and citizenship rights is, therefore, complex. Human rights, such as the *Universal Declaration of Human Rights*, are moral statements which suggest what should be but they do not have the force of law in any country to ensure that what is desirable is actually achieved. Hence, it is with the struggle for citizenship rights that this analysis must commence.

After the crisis, the new earth, the democratic society, appears to be going to arrive as a result of a number of factors – one of which is the promise of more education, especially of that liberal, cultural form that enriches the lives of the people. Education is a human right, according to that famous declaration, but it is not a citizenship right until granted by the state. It may become a citizenship right and if the right to education is not only enacted but funded, it may become part of a basis for building a new democratic state, in which able, thinking human beings are to play their part – even a part of engaging in the struggle for even more rights to be granted. Consequently, there is a sense in which education is both part of the promise and an element in the means to its fulfilment. It is part of the promise of participative citizenship in democratic society.

AFTER THE CRISIS – THE PROMISE

In this section it is suggested that the state functions with two different sets of forces operating simultaneously but sometimes in apparently conflicting ways. First of all there is a sense of national unity – that all citizens are equal members of society and have equal rights but, second, within the state there are opposing interests so that there are the rulers and the ruled and they appear to be struggling against each other in order to achieve their own ends. Hence, the sense of nationalism unites a people, but the struggles of conflicting interests divide them.

Part of the struggle between the rulers and the ruled is to achieve a greater share in the state's resources and the rights that citizens are granted might be said to fall into three distinct categories – civil, political and social (Marshall, 1950). In a later analysis Giddens (1985) substitutes economic rights for social rights, but this tends to concentrate the areas of struggle in such a way as to suggest that it is only a class struggle, and this is something that is too narrow. Held (1989: 171) has summarised Giddens' position thus: 'class conflict has been and remains the medium of extension of citizenship rights and the basis of ... polyarchy and the welfare state'. But Marx actually paid little attention to the nation state or to nationalism, and when he did it was to treat the latter 'as some kind of masked expression of the interests of the dominant class' (Giddens, 1985: 213). Held (1989) himself, however, is at pains to suggest that neither Giddens nor Marshall have really considered all the aspects of citizenship rights, suggesting that the struggle of women, ethnic minorities, etc., have all got to be considered within this context and this is far broader than merely the interests of class; indeed, it may be the interests of a middle-class group! Indeed, a part of the history of radical adult education has been, and still is (Lovett, 1988), within this struggle which will be discussed more fully in the next chapter.

While, Giddens (1985) has argued that citizenship rights tend to be granted after a class struggle, he (1989) certainly does not deny that Held's position is valid, and claims that it still fits within his analysis. But once he acknowledges that there are interest groups other than class who also struggle for recognition, there is a sense in which he has to admit that the Marxist analysis is too narrow and that the struggle may well be between the ruling group and interest groups. If this is the case, then Turner (1988) may be correct when he suggests that it is in status politics rather than class politics that this struggle occurs.

The positions demonstrated in the two post-revolutionary situations can be accounted for by the idea that society functions through struggle and tension, either within the laws of the land or in the case of extreme situations outside of the lawful procedure, between those who rule and a variety of interest groups who are ruled. Such groups, if they are successful, gain additional citizenship rights for all or some of the people. Hence, it is possible to see that in the two cases in which there was a successful revolution, the granting of additional citizenship rights in terms of additional education is almost a natural outcome. But the same argument cannot be applied to either the sentiments expressed in A.L. Smith's letter of 1919 (Smith (1919)), or to the duties laid upon local education authorities as a result of the 1944 Education Act. The struggle between oppressed and oppressors is insufficient to account for this.

Giddens (1989: 270) is also clear that the 'development of citizenship rights has been strongly influenced by the impact of war'. Nisbet (1986: 44) goes even further when he claims that with the revolutionary armies 'war became the crusade for freedom, equality and fraternity', and this approach certainly fits into the situation of the other two examples earlier in this chapter. There are a variety of reasons why this should be, and it would not be difficult to find other examples of this occurring. Barbalet (1988: 37) writes:

> The idea that warfare promotes citizenship, which has come to be widely accepted, is based on at least three propositions. In order to wage war states require the commitment of their populations, and this can be bought with an extension of their citizenship. Secondly warfare promotes social change through mass mobilization and state intervention; and under these con-

ditions there emerges a new appreciation of collective and shared responsibility and the means are created whereby meaningful participation in the nation community can be achieved through the expansion of citizenship, especially social citizenship. That is, in warfare people come to realize that if the dangers a country faces are to be shared, then its resources should also be shared. Finally, warfare promotes full employment and tight labour markets. Under these circumstances labour struggles are likely to put great pressure on employers and government and lead to gains for labour, including an expansion of citizenship rights.

After the crisis, or even during it, when there is a strong sense of national unity governments make their offers to the people – part of which is a promise of more educational opportunity – to build a new democratic society. Indeed, the state does not necessarily need to be successful in the conflict in order for the rights to be granted – they might be even more forthcoming in times of defeat, for governments have an even greater need of the commitment of the populace. As Barbalet (1988: 37) points out Austria, Finland, Germany, Italy, Japan and Sweden have all established their democracies in defeat. Indeed, Therborn (1977, cited in Barbalet, 1988) discusses 17 different countries which established their democratic rule as a result of defeat in war.

Both the sentiments of the 1919 Report and the 1944 Statute reflect the fact that after the war a people who had suffered together and fought together would together build a new nation. All the people would have the opportunity of life enriching adult education. The nation would be one in which the democratic rights of the people would be enshrined in the laws of the land. After the crisis comes the promise of a new society and one element of that promise is the provision of education for all – part of a Welfare State provision.

But society not only functions according to the spirit of nationalism and in the interests of the nation; it is also held together by struggle between competing interests. After the crisis is over the spirit of nationalism dies away a little and the interests of the groups re-assert themselves. The promise might have been made, as it was in 1919, but it did not mean that it actually had to materialise. In 1944 it was enacted, but it does not mean that the rights granted were irrevocable. Social conditions change and the struggle resumes. Held (1989: 175) makes this point clearly:

The autonomy of the citizen can be represented by that bundle of rights which the individuals can enjoy as a result of their status as 'free and equal' members of that society. And to unpack the domain of rights is to unpack both the rights that the citizens formally enjoy and the conditions under which citizens' rights are actually realized or enacted. Only this 'double focus' makes it possible to grasp the degrees of autonomy, interdependence and constraint, that citizens face in the societies in which they live.

That is that the promise does not automatically result in an enactment and even if there is an enactment in law it does not mean that the process is irreversible, and the struggle is not over! Only when the elite is threatened, either by an outside foe, or by another internal elite group seeking power at the time of elections, or from within by the struggle of the different groups which seek their rights, is it prepared to extend those citizenship rights – and then it is as a temporary measure, an expediency, and when the conditions change those rights might well be threatened again. Indeed, Giddens (1985: 205)) makes the point that even in the granting of rights the state still retains the powers of surveillance, so that there is still control, although it is a dialectic of control throughout the struggle.

AFTER THE PROMISE – THE STRUGGLE

Thus it may be seen from the above argument that from a successful struggle by specific interest groups, which might be regarded as a form of *particularism*, social rights might be gained. Additionally, when the spirit of national unity is prevalent at such times as crisis and war, a form of *nationalism*, then the rulers also grant or promise additional rights. Consequently, it might be asked whether there are any other times when such rights might be granted. There is perhaps one more period when such rights are forthcoming and this is during those brief periods of romanticism, such as the late 1960s and early 1970s in the West, when human rights and individual freedoms formed a major concern for many people. During periods of romanticism, almost *universalism*, when the boundaries between peoples seem artificial, are probably the only other times when civil rights are likely to be extended. Periods such as this might occur in times of economic well-being for a country, when the elite considers that there are sufficient resources to spread them more widely around the citizenship. However, in the latter two instances, the period when the rights are likely to be promised or granted are brief and then the feeling of unity between peoples gradually disappears and the period of conflict and struggle between competing interests resumes. Often the governing party seeks to persuade the people that the policies it is enacting are in the national interest, which is often no more than a convenient way of presenting its own interest to a people with whom it is in covert conflict – but the extent of that conflict will always depend upon the type of government in power.

Two points emerge from this that have to be taken into consideration: first, governments themselves represent interests and so it depends upon whose interests the government emphasises as to whether those promises will be fulfilled or those laws retained and, second, the apparatuses of state are not neutral and will nearly always be used by the government to control the people and to ensure that its policies are enacted. Hence, the extent of the struggle depends entirely upon the complexion of the government in power.

In some countries of the world, such as parts of Scandinavia, where the governments have been notably more democratic, the opportunities for adult education and other forms of civil right have been extensive. Governments are prepared to make available state funds for the benefit of adult study, often irrespective of the subject being studied. The Study Circle movement, for instance, is government-funded and yet it might mean that a more vocal opposition emerges, certainly a more informed populace exists as a result. In countries like this, the struggle for new rights still exists and adult education still has a major role to play – and now education is one of the means of achieving that new earth – people receive that life-enriching education which Alanen (1988: 2), in describing the spirit of adult education in Finland, suggests as 'the overall development of personality in the spirit of humanity'. This depicts something of the Scandinavian approach to adult education, although he does indicate that perhaps it is changing a little. This is precisely what Nordhaug (1986: 53–4) also notes is happening in Norway at the present time, for as new civil rights groups arise there is little or no financial support for their educational activities, although there is still generous support for other adult education groups. These grassroots interests groups have not won their *particularist* struggle against the rulers and so, even in an enlightened democratic Scandinavian country the struggles continue.

However, it is not merely a matter of the struggle continuing with the oppressed gaining ground inevitably in their struggles for rights – the rulers are also engaged in the struggle, not only defending their position, but also seeking to claw back ground that they have previously conceded. The way that the rulers seek to prevent grassroots groups gaining their rights was illustrated in the case of Norway – by the control of finance. Such an approach has been employed by the New Right in the United Kingdom in the recent White Paper on Further Education. The significance of the approach of the New Right has been to withdraw financial subsidy and then to allow rights to wither away as they have become dependent upon the forces of the market. The 1944 Statute about providing further education has not been challenged, but with less financial support fees have risen and some people have not been able to afford liberal adult education – whilst adult education providers are spending increasing amounts of time trying to find courses that can be sold to industry and commerce, etc. in order to help support some of the now non-financially viable liberal adult education courses. Even more, in certain further education courses, political discussions have been forbidden and education treated as a training process fitting students for the world of work but not for their civil role.

In addition, new social movements are appearing such as the ecological movement, feminism, peace movement, etc. and there is no financial support for their educational activities. These movements who are campaigning for civil rights have received little or no support from any statutory body in their struggles but they are often presented as deviant groups who are situated at the periphery of society having some strange but often ill-conceived ideas. They seek to educate the people but sometimes their activities are not welcomed in adult education programmes – for instance, peace studies are regarded by some politicians as communist-inspired and to be avoided, whilst war studies *is* a subject worthy of study! It may be seen that it is easy to move from citizenship rights to interests, which is the theme of the following chapter, so that this aspect will not be considered further here.

The struggle continues and education is both an element in the struggle and also a right to be won. The movement exercises an educative function and for so long as it seems that it might be possible to win the social right the movement remains reformist and educative. However, if the cause seems hopeless, then more drastic measures may be resorted to and the educative function ceases to occupy such a prominent place in the activities.

A BILL OF RIGHTS FOR THE ADULT LEARNER

On 21 February 1991 the board of directors of the Coalition of Adult Education Organisations, 26 national adult education associations and groups in the United States published a Bill of Rights for the Adult Learner:

A democratic nation is made possible through the efforts of a knowledgeable populace actively committed to the general welfare and alert to the opportunities for personal growth and development. Essential for realising this commitment is the availability of a wide variety of adult and continuing education opportunities. The institutions and agencies of a democratic society will strive to assure that the following rights are possessed by all who have adult responsibilities and who seek to learn in any setting.

- The right to learn regardless of age, gender, colour, ethnic or linguistic background, marital status, the presence of dependants, disability, or financial circumstances.
- The right of equal opportunity for access to relevant learning opportunities throughout life.
- The right to educational leave from employment for general, as well as vocational or professional, education.
- The right to financial aid and educational services at levels comparable to those provided for younger or full-time learners.
- The right to encouragement and support in learning subject matter that the learner believes will lead to growth and self-actualization.
- The right to a learning environment suitable for adults to include appropriate instructional materials, media and facilities.
- The right to have relevant prior experiential learning evaluated and, where appropriate, recognised for academic credit toward a degree or credential.
- The right to participate or be appropriately represented in planning or selecting learning activities in which the learner is engaged.
- The right to be taught by qualified and competent instructors who possess appropriate subject-matter qualifications, as

well as knowledge and skill relating to the instructional needs of adults.

- The right to academic support resources, including instructional technology, that can make self-directed learning or distance learning possible.
- The right to dependant care and related structures of social support.
- The right to individualized information and guidance leading toward further study.

(*Adults Learning*, vol. 3, no.4, 1991: 106)

The above statement is, naturally, an idealistic statement of what those who lead the adult education organisations in the United States would like to achieve. Few of the 'rights' are actually enacted in law anywhere in the world – the exceptions include the right to paid educational leave in some countries and then only for specific educational opportunities, and the financial support made available by some Scandinavian countries for the Study Circles.

The costs of this provision would be enormous and however laudable the intention of the statement, minimum statists would argue that in order to acquire such revenue the state would have to tax the wealthy extremely heavily and such an intervention is an infringement of their rights. Indeed, they could argue that this would be unfair to the wealthy, even immoral. Consequently, this cannot be accepted as a basis for the educational rights of the citizen. Marxists might well contest this statement also, but for different reasons; since they might claim that to increase the formal educational provision in this way merely gives more power to the state apparatus of the education of adults, and this in turn results in the the powers of the state being strengthened by the hegemonic process of education.

Clearly then this statement would not receive universal assent from all the citizens of any country and it would be difficult to treat such statements as unequivocal citizen rights, but rather to regard this and similar claims as expressions of interest by a coalition of educational interest groups. As such, it becomes part of the struggle to gain more rights for the people from those individuals who control the state.

CONCLUSIONS

The thesis of this chapter is that the education of adults, especially in its liberal and cultural form, may be regarded as a social or a citizenship right. But it is not one which is conceded by the state without a struggle. By its very nature the state exists in tension and conflict – if the conflict is external and there is war then the elite needs the populace to support the state and so offer the people an extension of their rights, as the feeling of *nationalism* prevails. Nationalism also prevails after revolutions, and the same promise of rights is made. Within the social system itself during peacetime, there is struggle between rulers and particular interest groups and within the *particularist* situation some rights may be granted if the elite feels threatened. Additionally, after romantic situations of *universalism* similar promises also appear to be made.

However, society always exists in tension, with competing interest groups struggling – but the elite is not static in this contest and it is always seeking their own interests which sometimes entails clawing back those rights that the people have been granted or won in previous situations. Yet always there is a utopian vision of a new society – a new heaven and a new earth – a time of peace when force does not prevail but moral concerns for all people rule. After the conflict this vision is more prevalent and the promise of education is made, but whether it is always granted in such generous measure as was promised must always depend upon the continued struggle – for that is the nature of society itself!

REFERENCES

Adults Learning (1991) 'Bill of rights for the adult learner', 3(4): 106.

Alanen, A. (1988) Efficient service and the professional ideal of adult educators', in *Adult Education in Finland* 25(4): 2–13.

Barbalet, J.M. (1988) *Citizenship*, Milton Keynes: Open University Press.

Dworkin, R. (1984) 'Rights as trumps', in J. Waldron (ed.) *Theories of Rights*, Oxford: Oxford University Press.

Frankena, W.K. (1963) *Ethics*, Englewood Cliffs, NJ: Prentice Hall.

Gewirth, A. (1984) 'Are there any absolute rights?', in J. Waldron (ed.) *Theories of Rights*, Oxford: Oxford University Press.

Giddens, A. (1985) *The Nation-State and Violence*, Cambridge: Polity Press.

——(1989) 'A reply to my critics', in D. Held and J. Thompson (eds) *Anthony Giddens and His Critics*, Cambridge: Cambridge University Press.

Held, D. (1989) 'Citizenship and autonomy', in D. Held and J. Thompson (eds) *Anthony Giddens and His Critics*, Cambridge: Cambridge University Press.

—— and Thompson, J. (eds) (1989) *Anthony Giddens and His Critics*, Cambridge: Cambridge University Press.

Lefort, C. (1988) *Democracy and Political Theory*, Cambridge: Polity Press.

Leirman, W. (1990) *History, Principles and Models of Permanent or Continuing Education*, unpublished paper, Leuven: University of Leuven.

Lovett, T. (ed.) (1988) *Radical Approaches to Adult Education: A Reader*, London: Routledge and Kegan Paul.

MacDonald, M. (1984) 'Natural rights', in J. Waldron (ed.) *Theories of Rights*, Oxford: Oxford University Press.

Marshall, T.H. (1950) *Class and Citizenship and Other Essays*, Cambridge: Cambridge University Press.

—— (1981) *The Right to Welfare and Other Essays*, London: Heinemann.

Nisbet, R. (1986) *Conservatism*, Milton Keynes: Open University Press.

Nordhaug, O. (1986) 'Adult education in the welfare state', in *International Journal of Lifelong Education*, 5(1): 45–57.

Nozick, R. (1974) *Anarchy, State, and Utopia*, Oxford: Basil Blackwell.

Smith, A.L. (Chairman) (1919) *The 1919 Report*, reprinted by University of Nottingham, Department of Adult Education.

Therborn, G. (1977) 'The rule of capital and the rise of democracy', in *The New Left Review* (103).

Turner, B.S. (1988) *Status*, Milton Keynes: Open University Press.

— (1990) 'Outline of a theory of citizenship', in *Sociology*, 24(2): 189–217.

United Nations (1948) *Universal Declaration of Human Rights*, United Nations: Office of Public Information.

Waldron, J. (ed.) (1984) *Theories of Rights*, Oxford: Oxford University Press.

White, A.R. (1984) *Rights*, Oxford: Clarendon Press.

Yao Zhongda (1987) 'Adult education theory and development in China', in C. Duke (ed.) *Adult Education: International Perspectives from China*, London: Croom Helm.

7

INTERESTS

The last chapter indicated on a number of occasions that interest is a significant concept in any political discourse on the education of adults and it also concluded with a statement of a Bill of Rights for the Adult Learner, but it was pointed out that this is not, at present, a matter of rights but an expression of interest. However, 'interest' is a term that has not occurred very frequently in the vocabulary of the education of adults although a very similar one, 'need', has. It is important in the first section of this chapter to discuss the two concepts and then to distinguish clearly between them. It will be suggested that one of the meanings of the latter term is a welfare one, whereas the former term relates much more easily to individual wishes and also to a broader idea of human benefit. It is recognised, therefore, that interests may be related to the theory of minimum state intervention although the implications of this are much more complex, whereas needs relate to welfare and state intervention. Thereafter, interests will be related to the idea of liberal adult education and, finally, the educative function of interest groups and social movements will be explored in relation to community education and radical adult education.

INTEREST AND NEED

The concept of interest is extremely complex, having a variety of possible definitions such as: a sense of curiosity or concern; a hobby or pursuit; a benefit or advantage; a share or a claim; a connection; the charge for borrowed money; a return on investment. Several of these are pertinent to this discussion, especially those which refer to a pursuit or hobby and to benefit or advantage. The former two indicate a reason why some people follow certain kinds of education and the

111

latter two might be seen to relate to social position and the extent to which certain actions in society are in the interests of the people. In this sense, the idea of interest relates closely to that of need, although it does not necessarily have to have quite the same welfare connotations.

The two concepts of interest and need are intimately related at the point of benefit or advantage as the following analysis in which both concepts are shown to be ideological, demonstrates. Since both are used in the education of adults this initial conclusion suggests that their use in the educational vocabulary requires considerable explication, so that the concept of interest is discussed initially and, thereafter, it is related to that of need.

It might be claimed that people are conscious of their own interests as a result of their perception of both themselves and their world. They think that they know what will benefit them. But is might also be argued that this consciousness is false since it has become distorted through the process of socialisation. Consequently, it is possible to argue that people may not always be fully aware of their own interests because their perceptions of reality have been distorted by the social processes which they have undergone. Hence, some people may not know what is in their best interests in every situation and so they may be liable to be misled on occasions. Indeed, human beings are fallible in a very uncertain world, and so there may be occasions when they are mistaken and in these cases they have to be informed of what is in their best interest. When, for instance, politicians claim that a law, or a decision, is in the national interest even though it clearly benefits some groups and penalises others in society, those who are being penalised may accept it as being beneficial, or at least necessary, even though they suffer as a result of it. In other words, the people may have a false perception of their own interests because they have learned non-reflectively to accept what those in authority tell them is apparently in their best interest, or at least apparently in the best interest of the nation, and so on. It is from a perspective similar to this that Marx's idea of false class consciousness arose. However, it is possible to argue that people are frequently more aware of their 'real' interests and, in the latter example, they simply but often silently recognise that politicians do not always present their cases truthfully.

Consequently, it is possible to understand the logic of the minimal state intervention argument since individuals are to be enabled to work out and achieve their own interests when the state does not intervene, rather than to respond to the often false claims that others make about their interests.

However, Geuss (1981: 54) suggests that the only way people will ever know their own real interests is for them to have perfect knowledge and perfect freedom; a utopian situation which is most unlikely to occur. Only in such a situation of knowing their own real interests might human authenticity be fully realised. Without perfect knowledge individuals might decide what is in their interest but not reach the most informed decision, although the extent to which this is false consciousness or merely ignorance is a matter for debate. Marxists, for instance, have claimed that people in the lower classes have had a false class consciousness because they have been socialised into accepting many of the cultural values and interpretations of reality which reflect the ideological domination of the upper classes, and radical feminists might consider that many other women with differing attitudes towards feminism have a false gender consciousness because they have been influenced by the dominant male culture.

Habermas (1987: 234), however, has dropped the idea of false class consciousness although he still employs the idea of false consciousness, which he regards as either 'collective or inter-psychic, in the form of ideologies or self-deceptions', and he considers that this is accompanied by restrictions that people experience as repressive. However, there is a major problem with the concept of 'falseness', since it implies that there is a 'true' or 'valid' class consciousness. This would imply that an unbiased cultural milieu exists; something which is not so, and consequently every consciousness is bound to be biased by its environment. As there can be no true or valid consciousness in this sense, every interpretation might be regarded as ideological – based upon the perceived interests of those who are making claims, and so on; and the use of words like 'true' and 'false' may be no more than a linguistic ploy to convey approval or disapproval of specific ideological interpretations of the world.

In a not dissimilar approach Sartre, who prefers not to consider the influence of the cultural upon the individual, deals with the concept of 'bad faith'. For him, bad faith occurs when people lie to themselves:

Bad faith then has in appearance the structure of falsehood. Only what changes everything is the fact that in bad faith it is from myself that I am hiding the truth. Thus the duality of the deceiver and the deceived does not exist here. Bad faith on the contrary implies in essence the unity of a *single* consciousness.

This does not imply that it cannot be conditioned ... like all other phenomena of human reality, ... [but] bad faith does not come from outside to human reality.

(Italics in original)
(Sartre, 1958: 49)

Sartre, then, considers that bad faith is a self-induced rather than a socially induced construct. But in another sense everybody's consciousness is true because it has developed as a result of what they actually experience, so that the knowledge that they have is their own so that they know their own interests. However, they still do not have perfect knowledge in order to decide what is in their best interest in every situation. Indeed, if people had perfect knowledge they would be gods! But this knowledge is the individuals' own perceptions of their interests – it is subjective and, to some extent based on their previous experiences. Incidentally, in specifying their own interests, people may claim that they need to achieve them. Hence, it is easy to see how the two terms become confused.

Need, as opposed to interest, is the more frequently used term in education, as the work of Maslow (1954), Bradshaw (1977) and others indicates. But it is not considered relevant to this discussion to expand upon their work here since the above arguments are just as applicable to any analysis of need as they are of interest, although need does carry with it certain positive moral overtones that interest does not. Interest gives some impression of self-seeking or self-fulfilment, whereas need carries the connotations that its satisfaction is imperative, or else that others have assessed what is in the immediate best interest of the people, which is the basis of social welfare. In addition, it is these connotations which demonstrate that it is being used in an ideological fashion. Hence people 'need' to have a high standard of living, and so on. Consequently, the problems with this latter term are at least as great as they are with the former, and maybe even greater! Like interest, need has no empirical basis but in this case it can always be judged as a deficit against some hypothetical norm. That norm might be perfect knowledge or it might be a greater or lesser degree of ignorance, but justifying norms is nearly always a problematic process since they are not empirical. Indeed, the process is always an ideological one, worked out within the context of power and the interests of the participants. Nevertheless, many educators might well undertake their needs assessment from a totally altruistic motive although this does not prevent it being either subjective or ideological. Not

114

everyone, however, has attributed such high motives to educators: Illich (1977: 15), for instance, has suggested that: 'Educators, for instance, tell society what must be learned, and are in a position to write off as valueless what has been learned outside of school.' He (1977: 22) goes on to claim that need is 'the fodder on which professions were fattened into dominance', so that he thinks that the prescription of needs results in power and wealth, in precisely the same manner as politicians employ the idea of interest. McKnight's attack (1977) on the professionals' prescription of needs is even more critical. Both of these authors wrote at a time when the professions were under attack and, indeed, they contributed to the decline in confidence that people had in professionals. Now management and consultants prescribe from perhaps a similar ideological basis, and no doubt before long their prescriptions will also be attacked as being ideological, as indeed they are! However, the point at issue here is that need is as ideological and subjective a concept as interest, so that the learning needs cannot be established empirically. From the perspective of the manager, for example, an employing organisation may be seen to have deficiencies that might be rectified if certain workers were able to perform functions that now they cannot. Therefore it is in the interests of organisational efficiency that individuals need to learn. From a personal perspective, however, individuals might need to learn certain things because it is perceived to be in their best interests so to do. Hence, the concept of need appears to have a similar basis to interests and it does not actually overcome any of the problems raised in the initial analysis.

Both interest and need, then, are terms that relate to subjective perceptions of the world, to consciousness or false consciousness, and also to power and ideology. In some situations people may know precisely what their interests are but in others they may have false perceptions. In some situations people may understand what is in the best interest of another, while in others they may be totally mistaken. However, there are situations when those who exercise power may use rhetoric without understanding or veracity in order to convince others that the prescription of the powerful is in the best interests of the powerless.

Habermas (1972), however, in an earlier work which he seems to have partially abandoned in more recent writings, employed the term 'interests' in a slightly different manner and it is important to see how he used the concept before moving on. He clearly accepts the idea that individuals develop within an objectified socio-cultural world and that there has been a break between the natural and cultural worlds. He is at pains to destroy the idea of an objective world which can be studied from a positivistic perspective. People, however, have cognitive interests, that is, interests which guide people's approach to reality, which are the 'mediators between life and knowledge' (Ottmann, 1982: 82) and relate directly to human experience. Habermas (1972: 313) writes:

> The specific viewpoints from which, with transcendental necessity, we apprehend reality ground three categories of possible knowledge: information that expands our power of technical control; interpretations that make possible the orientation of action within common traditions; and analyses that free consciousness from its dependence on hypostasized powers. These viewpoints originate in the interest structure of a species that is linked in its roots to definite means of social organization: work, language and power.

Hence, Habermas postulated three forms of interest: the technical cognitive interest of the empirical-analytic sciences, the practical one of the historical-hermeneutical sciences and the emancipatory one grounded in psychoanalysis and critical theory. Only in the final form does self-reflection occur that can emancipate the thinker, or produce reflective learning, which might be threatening to those who exercise power. For Habermas, the critical self-reflection occurs as a result of psychoanalysis rather than from any sense of experience of pluralism. He (1972: 223) undertook a full analysis of Freud's work, especially that on dreams and concluded that: 'The restricting agency that controls speech and action by day slackens its domination during sleep because it can rely on the suspension of motor activity. We can assume that this agency suppresses motives of actions.' Hence, psychoanalysis overcomes blocks in the consciousness and penetrates false objectifications, so that 'analytic knowledge is self-reflection' (p.233). Indeed, the ancients used to believe that dreams reveal the truth! Habermas (p.287), however, goes on to claim that:

> In the case of an objectivation whose power is based only on the subject not recognizing itself in it as its other, knowing it in the act of self-reflection is immediately identical with the interest in knowledge, namely in emancipation from that power.

Unlike Marx, whom he thinks does not extend his theory sufficiently, Habermas concludes that Freud has provided a basis for understanding false consciousness and a way by which individuals can be emancipated from it through analysis. Habermas was clearly trying to get outside of the problems raised by the ideas of false consciousness and the possible inability of people to know their own interests. He is trying to show how the natural processes through which people suppress their understanding of their own experiences and distort their own biographies could be revealed through psychoanalysis and self-reflection. Hence, he has apparently provided a logical basis for a form of reflective learning, and while he has highlighted some important aspects of psychoanalysis his claims for it might be too sweeping. Naturally, he has been criticised strongly for this approach, (see McCarthy, 1981; Thompson and Held, 1982 *inter alia*), especially for his claim that in self-reflection knowledge and interest are identical since, as Geuss (1981) pointed out, true interests can only be known when absolute knowledge is gained and psychoanalysis cannot produce that! Habermas has adapted and extended this analysis in his formulation of a theory of communicative action. It was, however, this earlier work that led to Mezirow (1981) introducing the idea of critical theory into adult learning, even though Mezirow has now utilised communicative action in his own theory of perspective transformation.

But it is through some form of reflective learning, claim some educators, that those who have developed false class or false gender consciousness, might be liberated, or emancipated, and it is upon this that Freire (1972a,1972b) concentrated. He (1972b: 75–6) wrote:

> 'Conscientization' is more than a simple *prise de conscience*. While it implies overcoming 'false consciousness', overcoming, that is, a semi-intransitive or naive transitive state of consciousness, it implies further the critical insertion of the conscientized person into a demythologized reality. This is why 'conscientization' is an unrealizable project for the Right. The Right is by its nature incapable of being utopian, and hence it cannot develop a form of cultural action which would bring about 'conscientization'.

Only through conscientisation can the people know their own interests and so they are empowered to act upon the world to change it. Freire claimed that when the people seek to change the world in their interests it is a process of humanising the world. Clearly such a claim reflected Freire's own ideological system, although he has subsequently ceased to use the concept of conscientisation since he recognised that it was an over-simple formulation for contemporary society and the role that the state plays in it. Unfortunately, Freire never really developed within a conceptual framework which incorporated the state, so that it is difficult to apply the idea of conscientisation to situations other than those which presuppose a Third-World form of society.

Both 'need' and 'interest' are ideological and relate to benefit or advantage in society. For instance, when resources are scarce, those who exercise power – politicians and the leaders of commerce and industry, tend to divert those resources towards themselves, even though they might endeavour to present their apparently rational argument in a distorted manner in order to try to convince other people that what they are actually doing is in the national interest, or in everybody's interest, etc. Perhaps the people are not as simple as the elite seems to assume! People more frequently know what is in their own interest, even though their knowledge might be limited. The more knowledge they have, however, the more likely they are to know precisely what they need, what is in their best interests and, above all, how to achieve it. However, they do not require a great deal of knowledge to know what they need and what is in their own interests at a more basic level!

Some forms of adult education have adopted a 'needs meeting approach', which refers to the social welfare education discussed earlier in this book. Adult educators, however, might do a disservice to the education of adults if they claim that everything that they do is needs meeting – for much of it is based upon interest. In this instance, however, individual interest refers to liberal adult education whereas much radical adult education relates more specifically to 'interest' in terms of advantage or benefit. Liberal adult education, however, demands minimal state intervention and radical adult education seeks to exert influence on the state to intervene in specific directions and in favour of certain sectors of society. These will be discussed in the following sections of this chapter.

INDIVIDUAL INTEREST AND LIBERAL ADULT EDUCATION

One of the criticisms levelled at adult education by Keddie (1980) was that it was based upon an individualist ideology. Indeed, the motivation that many students have had in studying beyond school has been precisely that of individual interest. People study because they are interested in a subject, or because they think that it is in their interests to do so. However, the former category, which Houle (1961) called the 'learning oriented learners', undertake their studies for no other reason than that they enjoy either the process of studying or in knowing the content of what they are learning. The rise of this form of adult education assumes that people rationally know their own interests and have the freedom from state and occupational intervention in order to study and satisfy them. This, then, is the liberal tradition in adult education, even though liberal education is a life-long concept. However, it is not quite this simple.

While liberal adult education is an interest-based leisure-time pursuit, it would be unwise to distinguish too sharply between non-vocational and vocational adult education, since Tough (1979) demonstrates that many adults' self-directed learning projects are vocationally inspired, and Sargant (1991) discovered a similar phenomenon in the United Kingdom. Additionally, there is considerable evidence to demonstrate that adults return to adult education out of interest long after their initial education has been completed and discover that they have talents that can also be used vocationally. At the same time, it is possible to view all non-vocational adult education from a social reformist perspective since its provision gives opportunity for some to have a second chance, and a first chance for others for whom school was not a first chance. In addition, it might provide opportunity for people who are at the lower end of the social hierarchy to learn more about how society operates and to discover that some of their taken-for-granted assumptions about it are distorted – in other words they might learn more about their real interests. Additionally, aspects of liberal adult education might be seen as responding to specific needs of some of the learners. In these senses, non-vocational adult education can be viewed as a democratically orientated state-provided welfare facility for those who have educational needs. However, it is hard, if not impossible, to measure the cost-effectiveness to the nation of this form of adult education provision.

Measuring cost-effectiveness in this manner, however, is an antithesis of liberalism itself. Arblaster (1984: 15) epitomises this position:

> Liberal individualism is both ontological and ethical. It involves seeing the individual as primary, as more 'real' or fundamental to human society and its institutions and structures. It involves attaching a higher moral value to the individual than to society

or to any collective group. In this way of thinking the individual comes *before* society in every sense. He is more real than society.

(*Italics* in original)

From this perspective, individuals are free, rational and able to act in their own interests. Consequently, they are able to pursue their learning interests in non-vocational adult education, even though the rationale for its provision might have been presented as reformist, or needs meeting, in nature. This, then, is a major conceptual problem for non-vocational adult education – is it a leisure-time pursuit for those who wish to satisfy their interests, or a welfare provision for the needy which has been largely usurped by those who wish to satisfy their interests? or is it a welfare provision for those who need opportunity to achieve their human potential through adult education? Certainly, it might be claimed that it was during the social reformist period of the 1960s that there was a growth in the state provision of adult education in the United Kingdom. This provision was, to a great extent, regarded as a welfare provision and in certain areas in the United Kingdom, such as the Inner London Education Authority, this appeared to be its predominant rationale. Clearly, one of the other outcomes of the 1960s was a new debate about the nature of liberalism, as the earlier discussions about Rawls (1971) and Nozick (1974) indicate. However, a common feature of state welfare provision, not only in adult education but in school education and health, etc. is that it tends to be used less by those who need it most! While liberal adult education has served both need and interest in recent years, the minimal state approach of right-wing governments coupled with the mechanism of the market under which liberal adult education has been increasingly forced to operate has resulted in its becoming more interest based and less welfare orientated than perhaps many adult educators would have wished.

Once non-vocational adult education is crudely viewed as an interest-based leisure-time pursuit, then those who enjoy it should pay for it themselves, according to the monetarist liberal philosophy of the New Right political forces, symbolised in the United Kingdom by the Conservative governments of Margaret Thatcher and, more recently, of John Major. One of the results of this policy is that it reinforces the leisure orientation in adult education and makes it more difficult for those for whom it is a welfare provision to participate.

Another, and perhaps even more significant, outcome of this process is that some people who might otherwise have learned more about their own real interests and how these might be achieved are denied the opportunity to do so since they cannot afford the increased fees of a self-financing service. Restricting the provision of liberal adult education has, therefore, anti-democratic consequences. It is another method of controlling the state apparatus of education, which might be regarded as a form of social engineering. In this instance it becomes more difficult for individuals, especially those who are at the lower end of the social spectrum, to use education as a vehicle of self achievement and also for them to learn about how the state operates and how they might achieve their own interest within it. However, one of the bases of the radical critique of liberal adult education lies in the fact that individuals might use this knowledge to better their own position in society through individual social mobility rather than work to change the structures of society. Indeed, it is self-evident that, while not powerless to initiate change in society, even committed individuals have less opportunity of exercising political pressure on the state than do pressure groups. Even so, there are many instances when individuals have come through the liberal adult education system and have become politically active in the interest of those whose needs are not being met.

Through the operation of the market, the state effectively defines liberal adult education as a leisure-time pursuit for those who can afford it and, by so doing, lessens the potentiality of its being an effective instrument through which those who need to know how to achieve their own interests may do so. This, then, is one of the paradoxical consequences of the success of those who worked so hard to make the provision of adult education a state responsibility. Governments often use the institutional structures of the state in pursuit of their own interests! Not all adult education, however, occurs within the state sector and the final section of this chapter explores the educative function of interest groups and social movements.

INTEREST GROUPS AND SOCIAL MOVEMENTS

As the earlier part of this chapter demonstrates, interests are not only individual but they are also social and community based. Groups of people may wish to express their own interests or even to work on behalf of other people's interests, and so interest groups arise. These are social movements but they often also have an educative function. They operate at local, national and international level and in some instances they take the form of community education (see Kirkwood and Kirkwood, 1989 *inter alia*), in others they are typified by the term radical adult education (see Lovett, 1988 *inter alia*) and internationally, there are organisations like the International Council for Adult Education (see Hall, 1986 *inter alia*). Additionally, Evans (1987) makes the point that adult education is itself a pressure group and adult educators do need to understand how the political system functions and to exploit it in order to perpetuate their own interests .

A variety of terms exist that reflect these different agencies, all of which endeavour to influence the process of social change in the direction of their own intersts through their activities, for example community movement, interest group, pressure group, non-governmental organisation, social movement. Some of these terms are similar while others carry different connotations, but all of them reflect the fact that people band together with a common interest in order to achieve some end. Perhaps the term 'interest group' best reflects the intention of this chapter whereas 'social movement' is the most frequently used term at the present.

As an historical phenomenon, Tilly (1984: 303, cited by Scott, 1992: 129) argues that social movements began in the nineteenth century, when people voluntarily committed themselves to a collective struggle to realise the aims of their own programme. It was at a time when pluralism was beginning to gain ground and, indeed, the existence of interest groups assumes a pluralist society and a liberal form of state. As such, interest groups did not seek political power for themselves but they endeavoured to influence the state in order to achieve the satisfaction of their own interests. Hence the terms 'pressure group' and 'interest group' have arisen. While Marxists have claimed that many such movements have been based on social class, it is not a perspective that is adopted here since some interest groups have high status in society (such as the British Medical Association) and the membership of social movements tends to be drawn from across the social spectrum and often the target of the groups is not the state but business and industry, etc. and even other interest groups. At the same time the significance of the workers' movement must not be overlooked. But many voluntary organisations have acted as pressure groups at different times in their history and other social movements currently have membership from a variety of social classes. Blondel (1966: 159) actually suggested that 'the representative system of government would neither be efficient nor really democratic without interest groups'. Some groups have protective aims, i.e. they exist to protect their members' interests, whilst others have more promotional intentions. It is largely among the latter that social movements are to be found.

Indeed, the history of adult education is itself the history of a social movement. In the first instance, seeking to secure educational opportunities for adults was itself a movement, as Kelly (1970) shows, and the fact that individuals are still working to achieve these aims illustrates that it still remains an interest group. Indeed, this movement has institutionalised and in many countries of the world there are non-governmental agencies concerned with the education of adults, such as the National Institute of Adult Continuing Education in England and Wales. Once interest groups have institutionalised they tend to assume a more protective function, as well as a promotional one. In some cases the government makes a financial contribution to the organisation although in most cases the organisations are free of governmental control. Indeed, the fear of the withdrawal of financial support may act as a constraining factor on some of the organisations' activities! Consequently, some organisations refuse donations and other forms of funding from state sources. Other non-governmental organisations act as interest groups seeking to influence the government, but they also seek to promote their interest through education. There is a wide variety of concerns which different groups endeavour to make government and the people aware, such as community needs and development, world peace, women's rights, the environment, the unemployed, the hungry and deprived of the Third World, and so on.

Smelser (1962) distinguished between two major types of collective behaviour: norm-orientated and value-orientated movements. The former, he defined as 'an attempt to restore, protect, modify, or create norms in the name of a generalised belief' (1962: 270) and he suggests that economic, educational, political and religious groups may have norm-orientated aims. The latter he (1962: 303) defined as 'a collective attempt to restore, protect, modify, or create values in the name of a collective belief' and he illustrates these by nationalism, religious messianism, utopian revolution, and so on. More recently, Rucht (1990, cited in Scott 1992: 143) has distinguished between instrumental/power-oriented and expressive/identity-oriented movements – the former being political and the latter cultural.

Scott (1992) suggests that these latter two types may reflect the way in which some social movements develop, with the expressive/cultural aspect emerging first and, if the movement is not successful, then it adopts a more instrumental/power oriented approach. For instance, many movements begin as interest groups seeking to make people

123

aware of the group's concerns and interests. The motive for seeking to educate people may be entirely expressive, although the educative approach might be viewed as a means of getting a private concern on to the public agenda. Education, then, might be an end in itself for some but it might actually be a means to an end for other groups.

Groups of this latter type can only exist in a permissive, or democratic, state. In some democratic and enlightened societies, such groups may be eligible for governmental funds in order to conduct their educational work. However, much of the work is conducted on a voluntary basis by groups especially formed for the purpose, or by other non-governmental organisations which regard it as part of their mission. Achievement of any political ends through this approach comes because the government responds to the direct representation of the interest group, or in response to an aroused public interest, or because one or other of the political parties adopts the cause and achieves power at a subsequent election.

It is interesting to note that the ecology movement is one of the few social movements that has also sought political power in a number of countries at both local and national government level. One of the distinguishing features of interest groups in earlier times was that they did not seek power, only to influence it (Blondel, 1966: 160).

While the interest group considers that it can achieve its ends by peaceful means, the educative function is at the forefront in its strategy, but if the ends seem unachievable the groups may adjust their methods and adopt a direct action approach. Then their actions are designed not so much to educate, but to be brought to the public's attention through media coverage – like the politician's photo opportunity, these actions are deliberately designed to bring their cause to public awareness. The democratic battle is represented to the viewing public by an interpretative media! In these instances, however, the groups may be characterised as instrumental/power-oriented. Initially, such public protests might assume a peaceful nature but in some cases, such as animal rights and some nationalistic movements, direct law-breaking action has become an element in bringing their interest or concern to public awareness, seeking to force a private interest on to the public agenda.

It will be seen that established groups exist to protect or to represent their members' interests while other movements exist to promote an interest, often on behalf of those who are unable to do it for themselves. One of the main techniques that such organisations employ is popular education. The power of education is to be seen in the democratic nature of society, where an informed public can influence the policies of government. Indeed, it was an informed public which Mill (1910: 285) advocated in *Representative Government*: 'The only thing which can justify reckoning one person's opinion as equivalent to more than one is individual mental superiority; and what is wanted is some approximate means of ascertaining that.'

Interest groups seek to employ education not merely in order to educate the people but also to influence government policy in relation to their own concerns. However, this is probably an inefficient method of influencing policy since by the time an issue comes to the public arena much of the policy has already been decided upon, so that a more effective method of influence is to be engaged in discussion with government in the early stages of policy formation. Governments, through the civil service, do take advice from interested parties and the more established the interest group or non-governmental organisation, the more likely it is to be consulted in these early stages. However, when this occurs the function of the interest group is purely political.

The whole of the above discussion on interest and the social presupposes a form of state that is responsive to people's expression of interest. Societies which have a form of democracy have usually allowed, although not always encouraged, the expression of interest. The minimal state has tended to arbitrate on the expression of competing interests whereas the reformist state has tended to intervene and redistribute wealth and opportunity in the interest of the less privileged. The New Right governments have more recently tended to discourage an active expression of interest, claiming that they have had a mandate to govern as a result of their election and so interest groups are interfering with their democratic mandate to govern. But it was noted earlier in this book that the New Right, whilst overtly espousing democratic ideals, has tended to be selective in those that have been practised.

CONCLUSION

This chapter started by examining the relationship between needs and interests; it showed that both are problematic concepts and that there tends to be a confusion between the two. Thereafter individual interest was shown to underlie the idea of liberal adult education, since it is based upon the assumption that adults are free and will act rationally in their own interest. Finally, it has examined the social dimension of interest in which groups of individuals try to better their own private interests and concerns put on the public agenda. This last aspect is a programme of change so that it is not surprising that it is regarded as radical adult education.

REFERENCES

Arblaster, A. (1984) *The Rise and Decline of Western Liberalism*, Oxford: Basil Blackwell.

Blondel, J. (1966) *Voters, Parties and Leaders*, Harmondsworth: Penguin.

Bradshaw, J. (1977) 'The concept of social need', in M. Fitzgerald, P. Halmos, J. Muncie and D. Zelchin (eds) *Welfare in Action*, London: Routledge and Kegan Paul in association with the Open University Press.

Evans, B. (1987) *Radical Adult Education: a Political Critique*, London: Croom Helm.

Freire, P. (1972a) *Pedagogy of the Oppressed*, Harmondsworth: Penguin.

—— (1972b) *Cultural Action for Freedom*, Harmondsworth: Penguin.

Geuss, R. (1981) *The Idea of Critical Theory*, Cambridge: Cambridge University Press.

Habermas, J. (1972) *Knowledge and Human Interests*, London: Heinemann.

—— (1987) *The Theory of Communicative Action*, vol 2, Cambridge: Polity Press.

Hall, B. (1986) 'The Role of NGOs in the field of adult education', in *Convergence*, XIX, No. 4.

Houle, C.O. (1961) *The Inquiring Mind*, Madison: University of Wisconsin Press.

Illich, I. (1977) 'Disabling professions', in I. Illich *Disabling Professions*, London: Marion Boyars.

Keddie, N. (1980) 'Adult education: an ideology of individualism', in J. Thompson (ed.) *Adult Education for a Change*, London: Heinemann.

Kelly, T. (1970) *A History of Adult Education in Great Britain*, Liverpool: Liverpool University Press.

Kirkwood, G. and Kirkwood, C. (1989) *Living Adult Education*, Milton Keynes: Open University Press.

Lovett, T. (ed.) (1988) *Radical Adult Education*, London: Routledge and Kegan Paul.

Maslow, A. (1954) *Motivation and Personality*, New York: Harper.

McCarthy, T. (1981) *The Critical Theory of Jürgen Habermas*, Cambridge, MA: MIT Press.

McKnight, J. (1977) 'Personalised service and disabling help,' in I. Illich, I.K. Zola, J. McKnight, J. Caplan and H. Shaiken (eds) *Disabling Professions*, London: Marion Boyars.

Mezirow, J. (1981) 'A critical theory of adult learning and education', in *Adult Education*, 31(1): Fall.

Mill, J.S. (1910) 'Representative government', in *Utilitarianism, Liberty and Repesentative Government*, London: J.M. Dent.

Nozick, R. (1974) *Anarchy, State and Utopia*, Oxford: Basil Blackwell.

Ottmann, H. (1982) 'Cognitive interests and self-reflection', in J. Thompson and D Held (eds) *Habermas: Critical Debates*, London: Macmillan.

Rawls, J. (1971) *A Theory of Justice*, Cambridge, MA: Belknap Press of Harvard University Press.

Rucht, D. (1990) 'The strategies and action repertoires of new movements', in R. Dalton and M. Kuecher (eds) *Challenging the Political Order*, Cambridge, Polity Press.

Sargant, N. (1991) *Learning and Leisure*, Leicester: NIACE.

Sartre, J.-P. (1958) *Being and Nothingness*, London: Routledge.

Scott, A. (1992) 'Political culture and social movements', in J. Allen, P. Braham and P. Lewis (eds) *Political and Economic Forms of Modernity*, Cambridge: Polity Press.

Smelser, N. (1962) *Theory of Collective Behaviour*, London: Routledge and Kegan Paul.

Thompson, J. and Held, D. (eds) (1982) *Habermas: Critical Debates*, London: Macmillan.

Tilly, C. (1984) 'Social movements and national politics', in C. Wright and S. Harding (eds) *Statemaking and Social Movements*, Ann Arbor: University of Michigan Press.

Tough, A. (1979) *The Adult's Learning Projects*, Toronto: OISE (2nd edition).

8

A CIVILISED SOCIETY

In the previous chapter it was suggested that many interest groups have an educative function and that some of these tend to be classified as manifestations of radical adult education. Nearly all of these groups function in civil society, although their purpose is, above all, to get their private interest placed on the public agenda. Each of these groups is trying to influence either national or local government to make policy and take action to create conditions that could result in what their members regard as a better world. However, it is to be argued in this chapter that a more just and civilised society can only be created, in which more people can enjoy the 'good life', when government intervenes in civil society and seeks to impose the conditions under which such a society can be established and maintained, so that this chapter might be regarded as an extension of the previous one. Government must intervene because the market is competitive and, while it adds wealth to society as a whole, it does not have the facility to become co-operative under any circumstances.

Such a society debars a proportion of the population from enjoying the fruits of civilised society, which makes that society less than fully civilised! However, any form of society which extends this privilege to all, or the vast majority, of the population appears to be contrary to the outcomes of the political agenda of the New Right governments, which have been seeking to reduce state intervention in civil society, so the political agenda itself needs questioning. At the same time, it is recognised that there are arguments from the New Right, from such writers as Hayek (1944) and Nozick (1974), which do have moral content and which have to be taken seriously.

The production of a just and civilised society cannot be left to market forces nor individual morality, despite the claims that morality is a personal thing which should be left to the charity of caring individuals. Civil society, at the present time does not have the mechanism to produce a fully civilised nor just society, and so it needs to be reformed. Indeed, this argument echoes Held's (1987) claim that reform is necessary for both state power and civil society (see Chapter 5). Since the market results inevitably in the survival of the fittest, the state needs to intervene in order to establish the necessary conditions in which those who are less strong or less competitive might also enjoy a just and civilised society.

In order to do this it is essential first to demonstrate that the market does need reforming and then to look at the ideas of justice and civilised society. The final section of the chapter examines the place of the education of adults in such a society and it will also be suggested that, among other things, the provision of education for adults and other cultural/educative institutions are symbols that society has achieved a level of civilisation.

THE MARKET

One of the central planks of governments of right wing persuasion has been to 'roll back' the mechanisms of state and to allow people freedom from government. The possibility of greater individual freedom is certainly a strength of this position for centralised planning does not encourage this to happen as Hayek (1944), among others, has claimed that individual freedom is best achieved through the mechanism of the market. The expense of administering the Welfare State bureaucracy is another reason for the desire to curtail the state's activities, and this has appeared even more excessive in a time of economic recession. Hence, it is necessary to analyse these mechanisms in order to show that, despite many advantages of both a personal and social nature, market forces are most unlikely to produce the basic conditions for the establishment of civilised and just society.

The market is 'a decentralized system of economic organisation in which the actions of individual buyers and sellers are co-ordinated through their common response to price "signals"' (Mann, 1983: 218). Thus there is competition between producers and retailers to sell and buyers to purchase and the price of the commodity is controlled by the market forces. This is Adam Smith's (1976) 'invisible hand', a mechanism which requires neither government intervention nor centralised planning. It is easy to understand the popularity of the market mechanism for a government apparently intent on reducing the vast bureaucratic mechanisms of state and its power in civil society.

More significantly, perhaps, it might be argued that the market mechanisms appear to be taken-for-granted 'common sense', so that such a policy seems to be regarded as perfectly reasonable. However, this position is much more complex than it appears on the surface for a number of reasons, including the fact that the modern mind actually has been moulded to think this way and, also, instrumental rationality is the form of rationality which is most dominant in contemporary society.

It was Simmel (1903) who first highlighted the way that metropolitan life was changing the way that people think. He (1971: 85) pointed out that the metropolitan mind had become more instrumental and technically rational, claiming that:

> The modern metropolis... is supplied almost entirely by production for the market, that is, for entirely unknown purchasers who never personally enter the producer's field of vision. Through this anonymity the interests of each party acquire an unmerciful matter-of-factness; and the intellectually calculating economic egoisms of both parties need not fear any deflection because of the imponderables of personal relationships.

Instrumentality, then, is Weber's purposive rationality – a form of rationality that is presented as if it were neutral and, as such, the highest form of rational reasoning. This assumption is reflected in the fact that it is referred to as technical rationality! It is this rationality which underlies human behaviour in the operations of the market, in which the conflict of interests is apparently resolved in a peaceful, almost automatic, manner. But as the New Right seeks to divest government of some of its role in civil society, it is being left to the market to determine the outcomes of many of the processes of civil society. Since the way the market operates is apparently rational, it is possible to represent this process as logical, common sense and good financial management. Consequently, not only do the workings of the market have to be examined, its underlying rationality needs to be understood.

Weber (1978) distinguished four different forms of rationality: purposive rationality (instrumental); value rationality (ethical); affectual rationality (through the affect and the emotional state); traditional rationality (through the habituation of long practice). The fact that Weber distinguishes these into four different forms of rationality indicates that he considered each had its own logic, distinct in some ways from the others. It follows from this that it is easy to regard each as an autonomous form of rationality which does not overlap with any other. Consequently, it is possible to separate them from each other and to apply them to different situations, so that the operation of the market might be assessed from a purposive rational perspective, personal behaviour treated as value rational, everyday life regarded from a traditional viewpoint, and so on. While this approach appears logical, these different forms of rationality can also be applied to an analysis of the same situation producing differing perceptions of the same phenomenon. Competing rationalities may, therefore, be adopted in order to analyse the same phenomenon in contemporary society, with some individuals utilising one approach and others another. The significant point about this is that both perspectives may be acceptable, correct and rational from their own viewpoint!

For instance, it is perfectly rational to regard the market as the most efficient method of production and exchange, or to treat it as wealth creating – without which there might be no 'good life', or as the major mechanism of innovation (Schumpeter, 1976), or as the means of preserving individual freedom (Hayek, 1944), or even as the main method of harmonising supply and demand, and so on. Each of these positions is, in its own way, a statement of purposive rationality. Additionally, they also illustrate some of the major social benefits of the market, whereas centralised planning restricts individual freedom and initiative, etc. But underlying the market is the fundamental idea of competition. With the competitive market, the 'weak go to the wall' and that the poor suffer while the rich get richer. Gorz (1985: 15), for instance, noted that:

> All reductions in public responsibility for social costs... accentuate social inequalities and, especially, the *visibility* of these inequalities: the brutal elimination of the less fortunate by the better-off, the violence of social relations in the struggle for scarce resources... the obscene privileges of wealth and power.

In fact, while this chapter was being finalised Archbishop William Carey (the Archbishop of Canterbury) was accused of attacking market capitalism because he claimed that the rich are getting richer and the poor poorer. During the same period that his speech was being discussed, the *Guardian* newspaper (12 May 1992) carried an article from the United States in which *Forbes 800* magazine was reported to be claiming that 407 chief executive officers paid themselves in excess of $1 million in 1991, with the highest salary being $75 million. It might, then be asked whether these chief executives merit such salaries? As long ago as 1977, Broom and Cushing (1977: 167 – cited in Phillips, 1986: 370) showed that 'company performance is not positively related to the total compensation paid to chief executive officers'. Their salary rewards are the result of their control over the market. But it is common in parts of America to be confronted by the request from someone begging passers-by to spare a dime for a meal. And in London, it has become increasingly common to see young people with placards carrying messages like – 'I am young, unemployed, homeless and need help'. (This was seen at Waterloo station in London just a few weeks before this chapter was written.) Politicians tell these people to get on their bikes and go and find a job – but some can hardly afford a meal, let alone a bike! And even if they could, there are precious few jobs to be found, partly because those affluent businessmen have been unable or unwilling to create them!

There has been something of a groundswell of public concern about the power of those who control the market and who apparently act only in their own interests, while the interests of the poor are not taken into consideration and the poor get poorer. This was evidenced in a leading article in the *Guardian* (12 May 1992) calling for a debate on the subject and from the Archbishop's own speech.

Interpreting the market from a purposive rationality perspective presents one picture but from a value rationality one another. Perhaps the most significant thing is that neither of them is necessarily wrong in itself. Each reflects a different perspective, but the dominant purposive rationality of the market is the one which appears the most rational and it is this which is generating a rich and a poor. It is generating the conditions of unrest in which the underclass might rebel because their interests are not being recognised or met. Riots occurred in the United States during the time that this chapter was being written and they have also occurred in the United Kingdom in recent years. Gorz (1985: 15) suggests that ultimately this process might result in 'the collapse of state legitimacy and of a social order based on the rule of law'.

Those who have the power to reward themselves with such unrealistic salaries and ensuing great wealth will no doubt experience the 'good life' and whatever high culture they might wish, but those who might be prepared to support a riot would hardly claim that their conditions are civilised or that they are experiencing the 'good life'. The wealthy, then, can support the political policies which roll back the state and leave the mechanisms of the market to control civil society, but those who are suffering as a result of the competitive mechanisms of the market might not be quite so supportive since those mechanisms do not operate in their interests. The purposive rationality of the market might be necessary to produce wealth but the morality of the market controlling every aspect of civil society is rationally open to question and debate.

The basis of the market is competition of interests. Ironically this gives rise to the very concern that Hobbes (1968: 185) expressed in 1651 when he pointed out that the first reason why people 'quarrel' is competition. It might then be argued that the competitive conditions of the market and for the control of scarce resources fosters an inherent instability because of the extreme inequalities it generates. Moreover, it would be hard to maintain that such a society of extreme wealth and poverty is either just or civilised. At the same time, competition is far from wholly immoral, as Kleinig (1982) shows. It produces people who are independent, free and autonomous – all valuable personal assets

This, then, is one of the dilemmas of the civil society being controlled by market forces. It can produce independent, free and creative people, as well as those who do not succeed in the competitive atmosphere. It can result in the good and civilised life for some who can afford it, or even for the many who benefit by the wealth that has been created by the system. However, not everyone can be a winner under such a system and the losers will not enjoy the fruits of such a society. They can only do that when it is made available to them, but significantly, the instrumental rationality of the market contains no place for providing the fruits of success in the competition to the losers! Supporters of non-interventionism by the state can, therefore, only call for the exercise of individual charity. But if Simmel is correct, then thought itself has become more instrumental, so that such calls might, but not always, fall on deaf ears.

However, if Hobbes and Gorz and others are correct, then it could be argued that these are the conditions under which the stability of society is sometimes put at risk. If this is the case, then it could be argued that it is just as rational to divert some of that wealth to further the civilising process in order to retain a stable society, but there appears to be no sign that this will occur. Alternatively, it could be argued that if this is not done voluntarily, it is necessary for the state to intervene in civil society and manage this fundamental contradiction between market capitalism and the production of a just and civilised society for everybody. In a similar manner, Offe (1984) argued that the state should intervene in civil society in order to manage any potential crisis that might arise between liberal democracy and capitalism, and introduce a Welfare State. However, civilised society is a different and wider concept than the Welfare State, although some aspects of the latter are incorporated into it.

CIVILISED SOCIETY

People in contemporary society are fond of celebrating civilisation: its dawn is frequently referred to, its history celebrated, its development traced and the assumption engendered that civilisation has arrived. It would be certainly fair to claim that by comparison with the Stone Age there has been a tremendous advance in the level of civilisation, and a great deal of this has occurred since the beginnings of modern capitalism and technological production (Keane, 1988). But, what will those people who inhabit this land think of today's humanity in another 5,000 years time, provided humankind manages to survive on the face of this earth for that long?

However, it would not be wise to base any argument on the assumption that as time passes humankind is becoming more civilised. Once there was a sense of optimism that the world was moving along a sequential path of history and that the end-product would be utopian in some way or other (see Chapter 9). But this form of optimism was dissipated as early as the First World War, shattered by the Second World War and the Holocaust (Bauman, 1989) and has been repeatedly destroyed ever since by humankind's perpetual inhumanity towards its own kind. Now the idea of contingency rather than a philosophy of linear history has assumed a priority. Optimism has disappeared in this apparently successful society of the 1990s, in which politicians of certain persuasions try desperately to convince the populace that there has been an economic miracle which has been achieved for the benefit of the people. They continue to try to persuade the electorate that they should be re-elected so that they can create the conditions for even more economic growth, since these are in the 'best' interest of the people.

The politicians still look to an economic paradise that they maintain market capitalism will produce. Certainly, technological production within a market framework will do many of the things that the economists claim, so that it is apparently logical and rational to continue along this path. But will it produce a just and civilised society for all of the people? Before this question can be answered, it is necessary to explore the meaning of the concept 'civilised' a little further.

According to *Collins English Dictionary*, civilisation has a number of meanings including: a human society that has highly developed material and spiritual resources and complex cultural, political and legal organisations; an advanced state in social development; intellectual, cultural and moral refinement; to bring out of savagery or barbarianism into a state characteristic of civilisation (as a verb); having a high state of culture and social development or cultured, polite (as an adjective).

It may be seen in the above definitions that civilised society is not merely a matter of reforming civil society, it also demands certain reforms of the state. Civilised society embraces both civil society and the state. However, it is important that much of the ensuing discussion concentrates upon civil society since the market operates in civil society, although the significance of the political elements will not be overlooked.

'Barbarianism' is not a word that is used frequently although it does occur in the above definitions; it is that state from which civilised society has evolved. According to *Collins English Dictionary*, it is: an uncivilised culture, insensitive, uncultured; a condition of being brutal, coarse and ignorant; to make barbaric, to destroy civilised culture (as a verb). But of course, it is generally assumed that society is now no longer barbaric and people are no longer insensitive. However, this latter assumption does need to be questioned because, as Simmel (1971: 88) claimed, those who live in the metropolis appear to small-town people as 'cold and heartless', and people are still homeless, today, etc. This might be one of the unfortunate results of the market; it has caused those who have been extremely successful to become insensitive to some of the conditions of hardship that also result from it. However, they still need to pacify those who are suffering, so that the claims of the powerful are couched in carefully prepared language, even though their deeds might deny their expressions of concern. (Many people do appear to be unmoved by the hardships of those who have not been successful in the market, although they are sometimes personally more concerned by some of the suffering, especially that caused by 'natural disaster' and in the Third World – but then it is personal charity that is regarded as the logical response to the problem rather than structural ones.)

It is clear that the type of conditions under which this form of civilised society might be achieved have occurred as a result of the technological production of modern capitalist society. Certainly, sufficient wealth now exists in modern western societies to enable the creation of a society in which these civilised ideals of intellectual, cultural and moral refinement and sophisticated material and spiritual resources might be made available to the great majority of the population. Additionally, it is maintained that the people should have the political responsibility to play their part in making decisions about how those resources are used. However, society still has some way to go before those civilised ideals can be achieved for all the people, although they are clearly attainable by those who have the material resources to purchase them on the market.

But can a society claim to be civilised if its cultural and moral refinements can only be experienced by the successful in the competitive market? Even culture and leisure have become commodities to be purchased, as Bauman (1992: 17) points out:

> As the interest of the state in culture faded (i.e. the relevance of culture to the reproduction of political power diminished), culture was coming under the orbit of another power the intellectuals could not measure up to – the market. Literature, visual arts, music – indeed, the whole sphere of the humanities – was gradually freed from the burden of carrying the ideological message, and ever more solidly set inside market-led consumption as entertainment. More and more the culture of consumer society was subordinated to the function of producing and reproducing skilful and eager consumers, rather than obedient and willing subjects of the state; in its new role, it had to conform to the needs and rules as defined, in practice if not in theory, by the consumer market.

Is success in the market a necessary prerequisite to enjoying the fruits of civilised society, whether they be high culture, education, or merely entertainment through the television (possibly soon to be 'pay-as-you-watch' in certain situations, provided that the satellite receiver for the relevant television programme has already been purchased!)? Perhaps not!

Moreover, while the definition of 'civilised' from the *Collins English Dictionary* mentions material resources, it does not expand on their distribution. However, it is difficult to regard a society as civilised when the resources are unjustly distributed throughout society without most of the people having some part in deciding upon their distribution. A civilised society must have a just social order, when even those who are losers in a competitive market system have certain rights. Many volumes have been written on the concept of justice, for example Rawls (1971), Nozick (1974), Gewirth (1978), Phillips (1986), Heller (1987), MacIntyre (1988), but the idea of a just social order which was discussed briefly in Chapter 3 will not be examined again here. Justice, however, has a universalistic element to it – it is something that should be experienced by the greatest number of people in society. Phillips (1986: 429), after a thorough examination of the work of Gewirth (1978), Rawls (1971) and Nozick (1974), claims that:

> In a just social order, there must be (a) welfare rights to the provision of such goods and services as free and comprehensive medical care and education, public housing, and guaranteed employment; plus (b) a redistribution of wealth and income to assure that everyone is able to obtain an adequate level of these and other necessary goods and services; and (c) the implementation of rectification policies to rectify earlier systematic injustices. After these stipulations have been met, (d) any inequalities that remain in the distribution of income and wealth are permissible if and only if they do not lead to concentrations of wealth that are demonstrably detrimental to some people's exercise of their generic rights.

Phillips is careful to point out that once people's necessities are provided for unequal distribution might follow thereafter, and so the principles of the market might still be free to operate in these situations. Not all of his conclusions are accepted here for the following reasons: there is no specific reference to political rights; the implementation of rectification policies appears to be impracticable; the statement reads as if people are to have things done to and for them – and this is one of the basic criticisms of the Welfare State – rather than that they should be given the opportunity to work and to be creative. In addition, Phillips, in common with a number of thinkers, for example Griffin (1987), treats education as a welfare provision although liberal adult education is certainly not always a matter of welfare provision but, as it was suggested earlier, it is often a cultural leisure time pursuit.

While Phillips' points are not all accepted, the above quotation was used here to illustrate the all-embracing nature of a just social order. While the market economy can produce sufficient material conditions to establish a just and civilised society, where the majority of people have the right to enjoy welfare, culture and leisure, the instrumental rationality of the market does not contain the mechanisms required to introduce the structural changes into society that would make this possible. It must be reiterated that many people who have wealth are personally concerned with and support charities, and that they live their private lives according to the principles of justice. But civilised society is not a matter of private morality but of public policy. It concerns the structures and procedures of both the state and civil society operating according to the principles of a moral rationality, and this is an antithesis of the rationality of the market. Hence, the civilising process will continue more effectively if the state intervenes and ensures that there are certain rules and regulations that govern the competitive market and its outcomes, so that some of its results, including welfare, culture and leisure, might be made available for all its citizens.

At the same time, there are other problems with this form of intervention since the state exercises power over a specific territory while the capital market is global. If the state seeks to control capital too rigidly within its own territory, investment will be transferred to another country having less rigid regulations, which reduces its opportunities to provide work and wealth creation for its citizens and, ultimately, reduces the potentiality for creating a civilised society at all. Consequently, it is only possible for political power to be exercised over capital if the political unit is geographically as large and as powerful as the capital enterprise, a reason for the development of the European economic community. But the larger the political unit the fewer opportunities which might exist for individuals to play a role in democratic political processes.

THE EDUCATION OF ADULTS AND CIVILISED SOCIETY

The final section of the chapter limits its discussion to the relationship between the civilising process and the education of adults, rather than examining all the broader issues mentioned above. Since the benefits of technological production are not being questioned it also omits any discussion about the necessary provision of vocational education in all its forms for all citizens whatever their social class, colour or gender. However, it is recognised that a strict division between it and traditional liberal and general education for adults is over-simple (Sargant, 1991) and that even where the provision exists there is not equal opportunity for all workers to benefit from it (Killeen and Bird,

1981). Additionally, it has been argued earlier that certain aspects of the education for adults might be regarded as welfare and others as leisure, but as the provision of both is regarded as part of the process of civilisation, they are linked together in this discussion. However, the relationship between adult education and the civilising process is rather complex, so that the following analysis contains three separate sections: adult education as an instrument in the process of change; education as a civilising process in itself; adult education as a symbol of civilised society.

Adult education as an instrument in the process of change

Traditionally adult education has regarded itself as a movement and there are two ways in which this movement has been active. First, as education – it has been a political interest group in its own right seeking to gain the right for working and underprivileged people to be educated so that they could play their role in society as adult human beings. Second – as the educative function of other interest groups, in the manner which was discussed in the previous chapter.

Throughout its history there have been many activists working in a variety of organisations, such as the churches and the trades unions, who have maintained that the working classes and underprivileged groups in society should have more educational opportunity. The success of their activities has resulted in the creation of many educational opportunities for working people, i.e. the Working Man's College, the Workers' Educational Association, Ruskin College, the Plebs League, Hillcroft College for women, etc. In addition, there are similar activists working to provide educational opportunities for people in the Third World, such as the literacy movement, education for development in Third World countries, health education, etc. Through these activities adult education has been both a political movement and an educational one trying to provide an opportunity for the people to be educated, so that they can play their part in making the society a better place in which to live. Freire understands education in precisely this way, although for him it has revolutionary implications: 'Human existence cannot be silent, nor can it be nourished by false words, but only by true ones, with which men transform the world. To exist, humanly, is to *name* the world, to change it (Freire, 1972: 60–1).

He continues on the same page to suggest that it is only in the dialogue that people humanise the world, that is that they might make it a more civilised place in which to live. In this work (Freire, 1972) Freire is concerned with making the Third World a more civilised place within which to live – and for some this is making these countries more like the West, as if it contains all the answers to their problems! There is also a conceptual conflict between modernisation and development. Some people regard modernisation as developing in the western direction – indeed, in Japan the word 'modern' actually refers to western. Development, by contrast, is when the people of the land have the freedom to develop in the direction that they desire – which should be the political right for citizens in their own society. Here two educational methods may be discovered, which Freire calls 'banking education' and 'problem-posing education' and which elsewhere has been called education from above and education of equals (Jarvis, 1985). In the former, those who are dominant seek to impose their knowledge and values upon the learners, whereas in the latter there is a dialogue when mutual learning between teachers and learners is facilitated in an exchange of knowledge and ideas – which is a more civilised educational process.

Second, there are those activists who seek to educate the world to understand their own aims and understanding of the world (see Chapter 7). It is these who are involved in the interest groups, such as Greenpeace, the peace movement, etc. They seek to educate the people. Interest groups use educational processes in order to make people aware that the world can be a more civilised place. While those movements are often referred to as radical adult education, they tend to be reformist rather than revolutionary. The use of the educative function is a symbol that the activists believe that the world can be changed peacefully through education, for if they did not they might resort to direct action. Radical adult education, is then, a symbol that the civilising process need not be revolutionary but can be peaceful, even civil! The history of revolution illustrates that it is an uncivil method by which to better the world – although there are times when it might be is the lesser of two evils, since not all political dictators or elites have showed concern about the people over whom they have exercised power.

Education as a civilising process

Education is more than a social movement, above all it is a process through which individuals are able to grow and develop their own humanity. Dewey (1916: 95) maintained that the education of children is a civilising process:

> The peculiarity of the human life is that man [*sic*] has to create himself by his own voluntary efforts; he has to make himself a truly moral, rational and free being. This creative effort is carried on by the educational activities of slow generations. Its acceleration depends upon men consciously striving to educate their successors not for the existing state of affairs but so as to make possible a future better humanity....

Dewey is concerned here not to create better living conditions but a better humanity. Paul Lengrand (1975: 139), echoes this sentiment for lifelong education:

> The accent is on the *human being*. The real education process concentrates not on a body of knowledge designated arbitrarily as the content of education, but on the needs of the human being, his [*sic*] aspirations and the living relations he maintains with the world of objects and persons. Education covers everything that can provide intellectual, aesthetic or spiritual substance for the individual and becomes an integral part of his being....

For Lengrand, then, the process of education is learning to appreciate those values which were described as symbols of civilisation. Becoming educated is becoming 'capable of delighting in a variety of pursuits and projects for their own sake and whose pursuit of them and general conduct of life is transformed by some degree of all round understanding and sensitivity' (Peters, 1977: 13).

For Dewey, Lengrand and Peters, among others, the process of becoming educated is one of acquiring some of those values which might be discovered in civilised society. In each of the above cases, existential values are seen to be significant although no one denies the importance of other forms of teaching and learning for vocational or instrumental purposes. Becoming educated, in this sense, is a civilising process.

Adult education as a symbol of civilised society

It will be recalled that *Collins English Dictionary* offered a variety of definitions such as:

> a human society that has highly developed material and spiritual

resources and a complex cultural, political and legal organisations; an advanced state in social development; intellectual, cultural and moral refinement; to bring out of savagery or barbarianism into a state characteristic of civilisation (as a verb); having a high state of culture and social development or cultured, polite (as an adjective).

When a society utilises some of its resources to provide the opportunities for all the people who wish to participate in the 'cultural, political and legal organisations' and to engage in 'intellectual, cultural and moral' pursuits then the symbols of a civilised society are beginning to appear. Rawls (1971: 107) suggested that:

resources for education [should] not be allotted solely or necessarily mainly according to their return as estimated in productive trained abilities, but also according to the worth in enriching the personal and social life of citizens, including here the less favored. As a society progresses the latter consideration becomes increasingly more important.

Elsewhere, he (p.101) suggests that:

the difference principle would allocate resources in education, say, to improve the long-term expectation of the less favored. If this end is attained by giving more attention to the better endowed, it is permissible; otherwise not. And in making this decision, the value of education should not be assessed in terms of economic efficiency and social welfare. Equally if not more important is the role of education in enabling a person to enjoy the culture of his [sic] society and to take part in its affairs, and in this way to provide for each individual a secure sense of his own worth.

This then is not the rationality of the market, but the value rationality of the just society. In this sense, the provision of adult education and also museums, libraries, all forms of musical expression and other cultural phenomena are symbols of a civilised society. If they are regarded as the rewards of success in the competitive market, then they are devalued, and society is that bit less civilised.

But it could be argued that it is only in this competitive society, when some people dominate over others, that opportunities for high culture emerge. After all the Greeks might not have produced their thinkers had they not been a leisured class. Veblen (1912: 235) claims that the influence of the leisure class is most clear in higher learning. However, conditions now exist when increasing numbers of people have more leisure so that more people have the time to participate in such pursuits, provided that they are available and affordable. To make them available at a price beyond the reach of many, except the most wealthy, is to make them a reward of the market.

CONCLUSIONS

At the present time the policies of the New Right are ones that are going to roll back the state and allow the market to dominate in all aspects of civil society. The market has many advantages which have to be recognised, so that such policies have a certain logic. At the same time, the instrumental rationality of the market precludes its creating the conditions in which a just and civilised society can emerge, despite its many apparent advantages. Hence, it is necessary for the state to intervene and create them, which is contrary to the current policies. Hence, it is essential that the different rational ways of viewing the market needs to be recognised and ways of resolving the contradictions between them explored. The aim should be of achieving a just and civilised society, something which does not lie beyond the bounds of possibility, although for some it may appear to be a utopian vision.

REFERENCES

Bauman, Z. (1989) *Modernity and the Holocaust*, Cambridge: Polity Press.
—— (1992) *Intimations of Post Modernity*, London: Routledge.
Broom, L. and Cushing, R. (1977) 'A modest test of an immodest theory: the functional theory of stratification', *American Sociological Review* 42: 157–69.
Collins (1979) *Collins English Dictionary*, London: Collins.
Dewey, J. (1916) *Democracy and Education*, New York: Free Press.
Freire, P. (1972) *Pedagogy of the Oppressed*, Harmondsworth: Penguin.
Gewirth, A. (1978) *Reason and Morality*, Chicago: Chicago University Press.
Gorz, A. (1985) *Paths to Paradise*, London: Pluto Press.
Griffin, C. (1987) *Adult Education as Social Policy*, London: Croom Helm.
Guardian, The (1992) 'More US chiefs earning $1m' 12 May.
—— (1992) 'Dr Carey's diagnosis' 12 May (leading article).
Hayek, F. (1944) *The Road to Serfdom*, London: ARK paperbacks (1988).
Held, D. (1987) *Models of Democracy*, Cambridge: Polity Press.
Heller, A. (1987) *Beyond Justice*, Oxford: Basil Blackwell.
Hobbes, T. (1968) *Leviathan*, Harmondsworth: Penguin (first published 1651).

Jarvis, P. (1985) *The Sociology of Adult and Continuing Education*, London: Croom Helm.

Keane, J. (1988) *Democracy and Civil Society*, London: Verso.

Killeen, J. and Bird, M. (1981) *Education and Work*, Leicester: National Institute of Adult Education.

Kleinig, J. (1982) *Philosophical Issues in Education*, London: Croom Helm.

Lengrand, P. (1975) *An Introduction to Lifelong Education*, London: Croom Helm.

MacIntyre, A. (1988) *Whose Justice? Which Rationality?* London: Duckworth.

Mann, M. (1983) *Student Encyclopedia of Sociology*, London: Macmillan.

Nozick, R. (1974) *Anarchy, State and Utopia*, Oxford: Basil Blackwell.

Offe, C. (1984) *Contradictions of the Welfare State*, London: Hutchinson.

Peters, R.S. (1977) *Education and the Education of Teachers*, London: Routledge and Kegan Paul.

Phillips, D. (1986) *Towards a Just Social Order*, Princeton: Princeton University Press.

Rawls, J. (1971) *A Theory of Justice*, Cambridge, MA: Belknap Press of Harvard University Press.

Sargant, N. (1991) *Learning and Leisure*, Leicester: NIACE.

Schumpeter, J. (1976) *Capitalism, Socialism and Democracy*, London: George Allen and Unwin.

Simmel, G. (1903) 'The metropolis and mental life', in K. Thompson and J. Tunstall (eds) *Sociological Perspectives*, Harmondsworth: Penguin in association with the Open University Press.

Smith, A. (1976) *An Inquiry into the Nature and Causes of the Wealth of Nations*, Oxford: Oxford University Press (first published 1776).

Veblen, T. (1912) *The Theory of the Leisure Class*, New York: Mentor.

Weber, M. (1978) *Economy and Society*, (2 vols) Berkeley: University of California Press.

9

ADULT EDUCATION AND UTOPIAN THOUGHT

The creation of a just and civilised society appears to be an almost utopian dream. Even the creation of a truly democratic society, Held's 'direct democracy' with his assertion that this is the 'end of politics' is utopian. Indeed, it is most significant that at the time of New Right domination, there has been a resurgence in utopian theorising (Gorz, 1985; Kumar 1987,1991; Levitas, 1990 *inter alia*) reflecting a 'desire for a better way of being (Levitas, 1990: 181), so that it is necessary to relate this type of thinking to some of the ideas of radical adult education and interest groups generally. The first two parts of this chapter explore some of the differing ideas about utopia while the final section relates these ideas to adult education thought, especially to the writings of Horton and Freire.

Utopia itself is a difficult concept to define. Nozick (1974: 294), without defining it, suggests that it 'must be, in some restricted sense, the best for all of us; the best world imaginable'. Levitas (1990: 1) opens her study by claiming that: 'Utopia is about how we would live and what kind of world we would live in if we could.... The construction of imaginary worlds, free from the difficulties that beset us in reality, takes place in any culture...'. She suggests that the idea of utopia embodies form, function and content and that any understanding of the term must embrace all three. Kumar (1991), however, defines it in terms of its function only, a point which Levitas (1992) disputes. In order to understand it, she (1990: 183) suggests that utopianism 'has as a precondition a disparity between socially constructed need and socially prescribed and actually available means of satisfaction', and she goes (1990: 191) to write:

Utopia expresses and explores what is desired; under certain conditions it also contains the hope that these desires may be

145

met in reality, rather than merely in fantasy. The essential element in utopia is not hope, but desire – the desire for a better way of being. It involves imagining a state of being in which the problems which actually confront us are removed or resolved, often, but not necessarily, through imagining a state of the world in which the scarcity gap is closed or the 'collective problem' solved.

She points out that this definition is analytic rather than descriptive, although it is hardly a conceptual definition. At the same time there have been many expressions of desire about creating at least a new earth throughout the history of utopian thought, and while not all that writing will be examined here, even if it were possible, a few of the significant writings will be mentioned. It is interesting to note, however, that one study was written especially for adult education classes, and, according to Levitas (1990: 20–1), that was Ross' *Utopias Old and New* (1938).

Utopia is a concept to be found everywhere and yet because it is imaginary it is nowhere. But it has found its place in political and religious writings and so the first two sections of this chapter will explore some of these briefly, although the distinction between political and religious is extremely arbitrary. The final section relates this discussion to adult education.

POLITICAL UTOPIAS

The concept of utopia as a political concept, Kumar (1991: 1) claims, really emerged in 1516 with the writing of Sir Thomas More, another point with which Levitas (1992) disagrees. Visions of a better world, an ideal city and even a paradise from which humankind emerged, appear to have been present in utopian literature for much longer. Utopian studies have highlighted the fact that the Judeo-Christian myths are not an exclusive cultural phenomenon. Kumar notes the fact that whilst Plato's *Republic* is a utopian study, it actually comes quite late in the development of Greek utopian thought. He suggests (1987: 3) that:

Utopian themes reach back to the earliest Greek writings. From Hesiod's *Works and Days*, of the early seventh century BC, came the canonical depiction of the Golden Age, the bitterly lamented age of Kronos' reign: when men 'lived as if they were gods, their hearts free from sorrow, and without hard work or pain'; when 'the fruitful earth yielded its abundant harvest to them of its own accord, and they lived in ease and peace upon their lands with many good things.'

Shades of the Garden of Eden! And so from the times of earliest recorded literature, the people looked back to a golden age but also looked forward to another. Before and after time, there is a utopian vision!

In the *Republic* there is an ideal city state, according to Plato, with its carefully thought out system of governance, and in Revelation there is also an ideal city. Kumar notes that the city was a significant concept in the development of utopian thought, since it was an escape from the natural world. He cites (1987: 5) Lewis Mumford who regarded the city as the first utopia since it expressed both humankind's escape from nature and the opportunity it presented to design its own perfection. Consequently, architecture has always played a major role in utopian thought. In the Middle Ages, with the beginnings of secularisation, even more utopian writings began to appear, including the fourteenth-century English poem *The Land of Cokaygne* where:

There are rivers broad and fine
Of oil, milk, honey and of wine

This then is the earthly paradise of the glutton mocking the life-style of the monastery. But, of course, the most influential piece of the Middle Ages is probably More's *Utopia*, which he viewed as an extension of the *Republic*, although there is also a humorous ambivalence about it. More expounds a form of social communism where all people are equal, where there is no money and everyone's education is the same. In *The Land of Cokagyne* and *Utopia* the visions are different reflecting their different origins, but in both instances the vision lies beyond the reality of everyday life and this points to one of the problems of the idea – it is not an easy concept to define (Levitas, 1990) and nor are its functions easy to determine.

Levitas regards utopianism as desire and this relates quite closely to the idea of wish fulfilment (Mannheim, 1936: 184–90). In a sense these perspectives approach the idea of interests, which was discussed earlier. Mannheim, however, treats the utopian element as the nature of the dominant wish and it is this which organises the way that people think: he considers that utopian ideas differ from ideological ones in as much as they break the bonds of the existing order whereas ideologies do not. The history of utopian writing finds a variety of different desires being fulfilled: from *The Land of Cokaygne* and *Big Rock Candy Mountain* (cited in Kumar 1987: 9) where food is in abundance, to the sexual freedom, to the abolition of property in Morris' *News from Nowhere* and Marx's classless society. In all of these the bonds with the existing social order have to be broken, either through revolution or merely through imagination. Mannheim's discussion on ideology is perhaps suspect in some ways (see Geuss, 1981 for a full discussion on ideology) since many of the writers who construct their own utopias are actually seeking to embody their own ideology in their utopian writing. Nevertheless, the distinction he draws in relation to the continuity with the social order is significant, differing just slightly in emphasis from that of Levitas. She seems to suggest that there is some possibility of social continuity in the fulfilment of the desire. Perhaps these two positions are not that far apart in as much as it might be theoretically possible for there to be social continuity but, in practice, it is most unlikely indeed. Mannheim goes on to distinguish four possible different types of utopian mentality: the orgiastic chiliasm of the Anabaptists; the liberal humanist ideal; the conservative idea; the socialist–communistic utopia. Mannheim (1936: 198) suggests that:

> For Chiliasm the spirit is a force which suffuses and expresses itself through us. For humanitarian liberalism it is that 'other realm' which, when absorbed in our moral conscience, inspires us. Ideas, not bare ecstasy, guided by the activity of the epoch... [give] itself over to the reconstruction of the world. This modern humanitarian idea radiated from the political realm into all spheres of cultural life culminating finally in the 'idealistic' philosophy is an attempt to achieve the highest attainable stage of self-consciousness.

This, the first of Mannheim's types, is discussed below within the framework of millenarianism. Mannheim locates the philosophy underlying the French Revolution in the humanitarian liberal tradition and this is certainly correct. The revolutionary violence, however, and the failure to achieve a utopian society in France indicates some of the problems of utopianism within such a liberal and rational tradition. It is also significant that Bauman (1992: 17) also suggests that the Holocaust occurred as a genuinely rational policy in the perceived but totally misguided understanding of the civilising processes by the Nazi party. Without doubt, the vast majority of those

148

who would espouse the humanitarian liberalism of utopian thought would regard the revolutionary actions, violence and massacres that occurred during the French Revolution as totally unacceptable, and are most likely appalled that the Holocaust could have ever occurred. They look to reformation rather than revolution, preferring to see a peaceful transition to a better world. It seems to them perfectly rational that people should live together in peace and harmony and that even those who exercise power should regard this as a logical end, especially since the holders of power often clothe their rhetoric in the language of service and equality. But with the revolutionary outcome of what may appear to be logical and fair propositions, the rhetoric may have become exposed. But the violent nature of change, even the discontinuity of the social system, also becomes more apparent, and this certainly appears to be closer to Mannheim's understanding and, as such, highlights some of the problems of his distinction. Indeed, it does point to the fact that it is a utopian vision and that it might not logically be expected to happen in the real world!

Mannheim (1936: 206) goes on to suggest that conservative mentality has no utopian vision although it gives rise to counter-utopias. He appears to be a little inconsistent here in as much as it would be possible for those who hold conservative positions, for example Hayek (1944), to have their own utopian conceptions. Hayek (1988), for instance, argues that there can be no freedom without several (private) property which is at the heart of the morality of civilisation. Indeed, Hayek actually wants to see the state rolled back so that individuals can be free. Freedom is, of course, one of the themes of the socialistic–communist utopia and significantly in some aspects of utopian thought the extreme right and the extreme left appear to converge. They both seek freedom for individuals, opportunity of individual self-fulfilment, and so on – but for one it can only be achieved through the retention of private property and the functioning of the market, whilst in the other it is claimed that private property is at the heart of the problem and should be abolished.

By contrast, in a rather prosaic analysis of utopia, Nozick (1974: 297–324) demonstrates that it is not realisable and he concludes that the minimal state embodies most of the practical ideals of utopian thought. Kumar (1987) suggests that anti-utopias are the distorted image of utopia and could only arise after utopian thought has appeared. In a sense, the writings of Hayek, Nozick and others, are attempts to demonstrate weaknesses in the socialist–communist elements in many utopian dreams, but by doing so they also express

149

something of their own ideals, and as such they must be part of any debate on utopianism and anti-utopianism.

Mannheim's final form of utopian thought, and one upon which this chapter will focus a little longer is the socialist–communistic one to be found in the writings of Morris and Marx, and more recently Gorz (1985), among others. From the previous discussion, it may be seen clearly that Marx was not unique in postulating a classless society, and he was by no means the first to write about a better world, but because he was such a fine scholar and successful political activist his writings were taken seriously and he has gained a large following. But many who have called their ideologies Marxist have expressed their own interpretations of his writings. Since he himself also changed his perspectives during his scholarly life, something that any scholar engaging in real debate must do, it is difficult, if not impossible, to determine an orthodox Marxism – see, for instance, Tucker (1972) for a discussion about whether there are two Marxisms, or one. Indeed, after Marx's death there has also been a variety of revisions of his thinking. But this is no different to that which occurred after the death of Christ and the proliferation of Christian sects all having a different interpretation of his message!

For the sake of clarity, brief summaries of both *The Communist Manifesto* and *News from Nowhere* follow in order to demonstrate the two positions. McKennan (1979: 44–50) summarises the former thus:

> *The Manifesto* (Marx and Engels, 1969) falls into four parts: the first provides a history of society since the Middle Ages as a class society and they describe the revolutionary nature of the proletariat which itself changed during this period; the second and third provide an overview of bourgeois literature devoted to socialism, including utopianism which indicate the yearnings of the people for a better society; the fourth indicates the attitudes of communists to various opposition parties. However, the point is that the workers of the world need to unite to overthrow the bourgeoisie because the classless society will not just appear. Indeed, even after the revolution there must first be a dictatorship of the proletariat which will rule during the period of social adjustment and then the need for a state would disappear, so that the state will wither away. At this point, the dictatorship of the proletariat could be abdicated and the people live in a classless society.

William Morris, a radical from the Romantic tradition, also produced a communist-type study, in this case a novel (1973), which embodied the socialist–communist ideal which Slapper (Coleman and O'Sullivan 1990: 35–42) summarises *News from Nowhere*.

> This is a novel depicting a utopian society in twenty-second century England, it is in the form of a dream in which William Morris finds himself in this utopian society. On seeking to cross the Thames by boat, the participant discovers that there is no need for money, that the waterman is helpful and acts as his guide, introducing him to this strange world. Morris discovers everybody helpful, that education is lifelong but existing without schooling, that the Houses of Parliament serve as a vegetable market and a 'storage place for manure' since there is now no state, that people only seek what they need and that there is no acquisition of wealth, no private property and no marriage as such although there are loving relationships. Finally, the vision dims and dies. However, before the Equality of Life period had commenced there had been a revolution and it was the workers who had organised themselves to strike and to fight against the rulers for what they regarded as right.

More recently, Gorz (1985) has also produced a utopian-type analysis, in which he recognises both that the idea of full employment in a welfare state is no longer practicable. He looks rather to a society where utopian insight becomes possible and he espouses a kibbutzim-type approach where there are three levels of work: macro-social work (for the survival of the community); micro-social activity (based at local level and more voluntary except where it relates to the basic needs of the community); and autonomous activity. For Gorz, leisure is now a more significant concept but he argues that people will want to be involved in socially useful work because it will be appealing to people. Gorz does not see the state withering away but pressurising people into conformity, although he does maintain that 'in theory, civil society – the fabric of real, lived social relations – should be the only source of law' (Gorz, 1985: 73).

In the novel and the political manifesto there are similar processes, the utopian position cannot be reached without some form of social discontinuity – the revolution will come and after that the state will wither away and the rational and basically good-working people assume control and, finally, create a situation where pure anarchy can reign – no chaos but total equality. In contrast, Gorz does not explain how his vision will be achieved and, as Keane (1988: 85–96) observes, there is a variety of other practical weaknesses with Gorz's formulation, and the state plays a small part in his utopian vision unlike these other thinkers.

RELIGIOUS UTOPIAS

Perhaps the vision of humankind, perfect and selfless in contradistinction to the idea of sin and evil is one of the most significant parts of the utopian vision. Another is the recognition that those who hold power will lay it down neither voluntarily nor easily but, instead of there being a revolution, other thinkers have postulated that the future lies in the hands of a divine power. The prophet tended both to denounce the present and then to announce the coming of a new age, of a new kingdom – the Kingdom of God. Christianity, certainly, and Judaism before it, has always been a very realistic faith – it has looked at the present world and seen its imperfections; it has then proclaimed the Kingdom of God rather than the kingdoms of humankind. Throughout the Old Testament, God was king in the heavens and His kingship would only be finally manifest when the 'Day of the Lord' came. This, however, gave rise to eschatological expectations and to the idea of the coming of a Messiah.

Christianity inherited many of these ideas – indeed the passage from the Revelation of St John the Divine where the writer 'saw a new heaven and a new earth' (Revelation 21: v.1) appeared first in the writings of the trito-Isaiah: 'For behold, I create new heavens and new earth' (Isaiah 65: v.17). In the New Testament, the theme of the Kingdom of God is quite central. In Christ's teaching, the Kingdom demands high ethical standards of living and a total religious commitment. In a sense, the Kingdom is about a way of life foreign to that discovered in ordinary daily living, but which appears to be both logical and realistic, so that it remains as both a promise and a possibility: it is both present and future.

It is, therefore, hardly surprising at a time when the early Christians were persecuted for their beliefs, and they were being persecuted during the time when the Revelation of St John the Divine was written, that the eschatological hope for the future played a significant part. From the beginnings of Christian scholarship, also, this theme has been discussed, with Augustine writing *City of God*, etc. and so the hope for a future has continued to the present day. Whenever people are persecuted and deprived of their rights as human beings these hopes apparently re-emerge and take hold of some of the adherents in a very significant manner. 'And I saw a new heaven and a new earth' was re-echoed in that famous speech of Martin Luther King – 'I have a dream...'. To the depressed and under-privileged of the world, the vision of a better world is something of a dream, a hope, hardly to be anticipated but most certainly to be prayed for!

Throughout the history of the Christian church this hope has always been present in some way: it has proclaimed the Kingdom; it has anticipated this eschatological future; it has proclaimed a new heaven and new earth on earth. The mainstream church has always sought to work in a reformist manner within the established social systems to make the Kingdom manifest, although there have been times in its history when this has not always been possible. It has been persecuted and ostracised and sidelined from the seats of power, but even then its hopes for a better world have not been destroyed. But those who have been relatively successful in the world have not always been willing to stand outside of it, and so mainstream Christianity has frequently proclaimed its message of a new Kingdom from within the systems of the world. It has had a prophetic role, which it has not always fulfilled with distinction. But it has both denounced and announced and when it has done so it has not always been popular for its proclamations.

But, the Christian church has not only attracted those people who have been successful or happy in the social systems of the world, it has attracted those who have been less successful, the lower classes and the colonised, and those who, for whatever reason, have wanted to change those social systems that have labelled them unsuccessful, and so on. Indeed, it is perhaps easier for them to embrace such a prophetic religious position if they have not achieved a great deal of economic, political or social success. For many of these, there has been little to lose and they have found it more easy to renounce and denounce the world, and these are among the many who have looked for a new heaven and a new earth – for some this has been a matter of trying to create a more perfect community on earth, while for others it has meant that their religion has been millenarian in nature since, apart from divine intervention, they could see no other way through which the world could be changed and things could be made better for them.

Some have created their communities and have tried to separate themselves from the world. They have treated it as an evil place and have tried to establish their own perfect society on earth. Many examples of this may be found throughout the history of the church, such as the Shakers, the Oneida Community, the Bruderhof (Whitworth, 1975). Others, such as the Church of the Latter Day Saints, have grown and become large and significant institutions, but many have been no more than small communities that have been established and existed for a generation or longer, seeking a better way of life on earth. In the same way, other sects have emerged that have looked at the world, considered it to have an evil system of government and a sinful life-style, but thought that nothing that they could do would change it apart from praying for divine intervention. Their members, therefore, have embraced their own forms of perfection, have announced that the end was nigh and that the the Lord would return to earth to administer judgment and justice and then establish a new heaven and a new earth, of which they would be a part. This is the message of the Pentecostal movement, the Jehovah's Witnesses and a variety of other sects who have proclaimed this same message throughout the history of Christianity. There have been many studies of these sects by sociologists of religion, both of historical and contemporary groups, and of those which have developed in the advanced countries but also of those that have emerged among primitive peoples, but this is not the place to explore them further (see, however, Wilson, 1967; Burridge, 1969; Needleman, 1970; Evans, 1973 *inter alia*).

There is quite a clear division within sociological studies of religious organisations between those which have embraced and worked in the world – defined as churches; and those which have rejected the ways of the world as evil and which have, consequently, looked for a better world, either today or tomorrow – defined as sects. Sociologists of religion studied these groups quite extensively especially in the 1960s and 1970s, as the books cited above illustrate, although this interest has broadened more recently. At the same time, however, the study of utopianism as such has grown and developed and perhaps this reflects something of the significance of these early sociological studies of religion, but it also illustrates the fact that society has changed and people are now beginning to question the direction in which it appears to be developing.

Apart from the religious groups who have tried to construct their own utopian communities, few thinkers appear to consider that utopia can actually be achieved through rational and logical progress – there must be some form of social discontinuity; either humankind can achieve the utopia through a revolution or else it will appear as a result of divine intervention. When there has been a revolution, however, utopia has not resulted – but still the vision presents itself as something that might be achieved and which has not yet happened. What then are the functions of utopian thought? Utopian writing serves at least three functions: first, it acts as a critique of contemporary society indicating that however high the standard of living, and so on, the present has not yet achieved perfection and that there are sets of values other than those embodied in materialistic capitalism. Second, it points to something more that lies beyond the present which is not really economic in nature, something which appears achievable and quite rational, although it has not yet appeared. Third, however, for those who feel that it can only come with divine intervention or in the after-life, it serves as a sedative offering the people hope in their despair and a sense that ultimate reality is fair and loving even if those who rule the present world appear to be uncaring and self-seeking (despite the fact that they would claim to be otherwise). However, the significance of these types of religious hope has declined as contemporary society has secularised. Indeed, the millenarian sects appear to be more illogical than ever in such a world of rational values. But perhaps, the socialist–communist utopian perspective approaches the religious one in many ways, without being classified as quite so irrational.

UTOPIANISM AND ADULT EDUCATION

Considering its history, it is not surprising that these ideas have also been prevalent in adult education thought. Utopian thinking has certainly been an element in the considerations of radical adult educators, like Myles Horton and Paulo Freire.

Like the prophet, Freire (1972b: 40) sees the pedagogue being involved in 'denunciation and annunciation' in a utopian manner. He continues thus:

Denunciation of a dehumanizing situation today increasingly demands precise scientific understanding of that situation. Likewise, the annunciation of its transformation increasing requires a theory of transforming action. However, either act by itself implies the transformation of the denounced reality or the establishment of that which is announced. Rather, as a moment

155

in an historical process, the announced reality is already present in the act of denunciation and annunciation .

That is why the utopian character of our educational theory and practice is as permanent as education itself which, for us, is cultural action. Its thrust toward denunciation and annunciation cannot be exhausted when the reality denounced today cedes its place tomorrow to a reality previously announced in the denunciation. When education is no longer utopian, that is, when it no longer embodies the dramatic unity of denunciation and annunciation, it is either the future has no more meaning for men, or because men are afraid to risk living the future as creative overcoming of the present, which has become old.

In this long passage, Freire's utopian vision is fully outlined and his idea of education as utopian fully expanded. Because Freire is utopian he has no conception of the state after the revolution in his writings and, indeed, although he regards his approach as revolutionary he never discusses how the revolution will occur. His approach is much more in accord with Christian utopian thinking, in which he sees education as an instrument in creating a better world.

In the dialogue between Freire and Myles Horton (Bell *et al.*, 1990) Horton discussed how he thought that perhaps the religious utopian groups had the answers he was seeking:

I thought maybe that's the answer, these utopian colonies, these communes, getting away from life, and kind of separating yourself and living your own life. I was attracted to it but I was very sceptical from the very beginning. It seemed to be too precious, too 'getting away' from things. I ended up visiting all the remains of communes in the United States – Oneida, Amana, New Harmony in Ohio.... I ended up concluding that they were just like I had already concluded – that a person shouldn't live within himself.... And I discarded utopian communities.... Finally, it just became very clear that I would never find what I was looking for. I was trying the wrong approach. The thing to do was just find a place, move in and start, and let it grow.

(Horton in Bell *et al.*, 1990: 52–3)

The Highlander Centre started when Horton recognised that the religious commune would not produce the new earth that he sought and that he had to work for change and just let the situation develop: citizenship schools, human rights, the rights of black people, the rights of the workers, etc. were all started in response to what Horton considered to be the needs of the situation. In many ways Highlander has helped to change the face of America. The vision remained, but the revolution was transformed into a lifetime's struggle for reformation in order to create a better world. In the same dialogue, Freire asked similar questions:

I asked myself why, why is it possible that some children should eat and some others don't.

It was too much for me to understand that, but when I think of that, I once again see how much I liked to know, to think, to ask questions, to imagine, to realize, and how much I see I've begun to build the dream I still have. That is, I've begun to dream with a different society.... I was, in fact, beginning to have a vision of a different kind of life, of a different kind of society – a society less unjust, more humanized....

(Bell *et al.*, 1990: 58)

For both Horton and Freire, some form of utopian vision has been a motivating factor in their adult education work – an ideology that drove them on, but is motivation the only place for utopianism in adult education?

Utopianism is more than just a motivating factor, however significant that has been in the lives of people such as Horton and Freire. E. P. Thompson wrote:

And in such an adventure two things happen: our habitual values (the 'commonsense' of bourgeois society) are thrown into disarray. And we enter Utopia's proper and new-found space: *the education of desire.* This is not the same as 'a moral education' towards a given end: it is rather, to open a way of aspiration, to 'teach desire to desire, to desire better, to desire more, and above all to desire in a different way'.

(Thompson, 1977: 790–1)

Utopian thought has been both a sedative and an inspiration – this is something of its paradoxical nature, so that the education of desire is not its only function, although it is one which adult educators must examine. Levitas (1990: 124) has nicely summed up this position:

the function of utopia, which is not just the expression, but the education of desire. Utopia entails not just the fictional depiction of a better society, but the assertion of a radically different set of values; these values are communicated indirectly through their implications for a whole way of life in order for utopia to operate at the level of experience, not merely cognition, encouraging the sense that it does not have to be like this, it could be otherwise. Utopia contradicts bourgeois common sense and facilitates a 'leap out of the kingdom of necessity into an imagined kingdom of freedom in which the desire may actually indicate choices or impose itself as need' (Thompson, 1977: 798–9).

(Levitas, 1990: 124)

However, as Levitas (1990: 124) has pointed out, there is no purpose in educating desire for its own sake, its outcome must be the realisation of utopia. But herein lies the problem, perhaps by its very nature it is unrealisable. Whilst it might have a transformative and emancipatory function for some people, such as Horton and Freire, Horton's realisation was that utopia will not happen so that he had to start where he was to make the world a better place.

No adult education course should have the education of a specific desire as its aim – that would be indoctrination – but courses might be organised about utopian thought and writing which are educational. Utopian thought, however, serves another function for education – there are other ways of communicating and enriching experience than just the rational, cognitive domain; its presence acts as a type of informal teacher from whom its message is occasionally caught. Indeed, human experience is more rich than just rational cognition, and utopian thought points education, especially with its recent emphases upon experiential learning and education for work and wealth production, to a much wider domain of community education and individual development, in which some types of learning may be transformative in the way that Mezirow (1991) indicates. It suggests also that future experience is to be made and discovered in the present, and that it is important not to take the values of the present for granted but to treat the taken-for-grantedness not just critically but problematically. Criticism is not sufficient, it is not sufficient merely to be a critical thinker, for there is a whole new world to be built and that demands creative and constructive thought, so that the education of adults might contribute positively to both the development of people and society.

REFERENCES

Bauman, Z. (1989) *Modernity and the Holocaust,* Cambridge: Polity Press.
—— (1992) *Intimations of Post Modernity,* London: Routledge.
Bell, B., Gaventa, J. and Peters, J. (eds) (1990) *We Make the Road by Walking,* Philadelphia: Temple University Press.
Burridge, M. (1969) *New Heaven, New Earth,* Oxford: Basil Blackwell.
Coleman, S. and O'Sullivan, P. (eds) (1990) *William Morris and News from Nowhere,* Bideford: Green Books.
Evans, C. (1973) *Cults of Unreason,* London: Harrap.
Freire, P. (1972) *Cultural Action for Freedom,* Harmondsworth: Penguin.
Geuss, R. (1981) *The Idea of Critical Theory,* Cambridge: Cambridge University Press.
Gorz, A. (1985) *Paths to Paradise,* London: Pluto Press.
Hayek, F.A. (1944) *The Road to Serfdom,* London: ARK Paperbacks (1986 edition).
—— (1988) *The Fatal Conceit,* London: Routledge (edited by W.W. Bartley III).
Held, D. (1987) *Models of Democracy,* Cambridge: Polity Press.
Keane, J. (1988) *Democracy and Civil Society,* London: Verso.
Kumar, K. (1987) *Utopia and Anti-Utopia in Modern Times,* Oxford: Basil Blackwell.
—— (1991) *Utopianism,* Milton Keynes: Open University Press.
Levitas, R. (1990) *The Concept of Utopia,* New York: Philip Allan.
— (1992) 'Review of *Utopia*' by K. Kumar in *Sociology,* 26(2): 355–6.
Mannheim, K. (1936) *Ideology and Utopia,* London: Routledge and Kegan Paul.
Marx, K. and Engels, F. (1969) *The Communist Manifesto,* (ed. A.J.P. Taylor), Harmondsworth: Penguin.
Mezirow, J. (1991) *Transformative Dimensions of Adult Learning,* San Francisco: Jossey Bass.
McKennan, D. (1979) *The Thought of Karl Marx,* London: Macmillan (2nd edition).
Morris, W. (1973) *News from Nowhere,* London: Lawrence and Wishart.
Needleman, J. (1970) *The New Religions,* London: Allen Lane, The Penguin Press.
Nozick, R. (1974) *Anarchy, State and Utopia,* Oxford: Blackwell.
Ross, H. (1938) *Utopias Old and New,* London: Nicholas and Watson.
Slapper, C. (1990) 'Synopsis of *News from Nowhere*' in Coleman and O'Sullivan (eds), *op. cit.*
Thompson, E.P. (1977) *William Morris: Romantic to Revolutionary,* London: Merlin Press.
Tucker, R. (1972) *Philosophy and Myth in Karl Marx,* Cambridge: Cambridge University Press (2nd edition).
Whitworth, J.M. (1975) *God's Blueprints,* London: Routledge and Kegan Paul.
Wilson, B.R. (ed.) (1967) *Patterns of Sectarianism,* London: Heinemann.

Quotations from the *Holy Bible* – Revised Standard Version.

INDEX